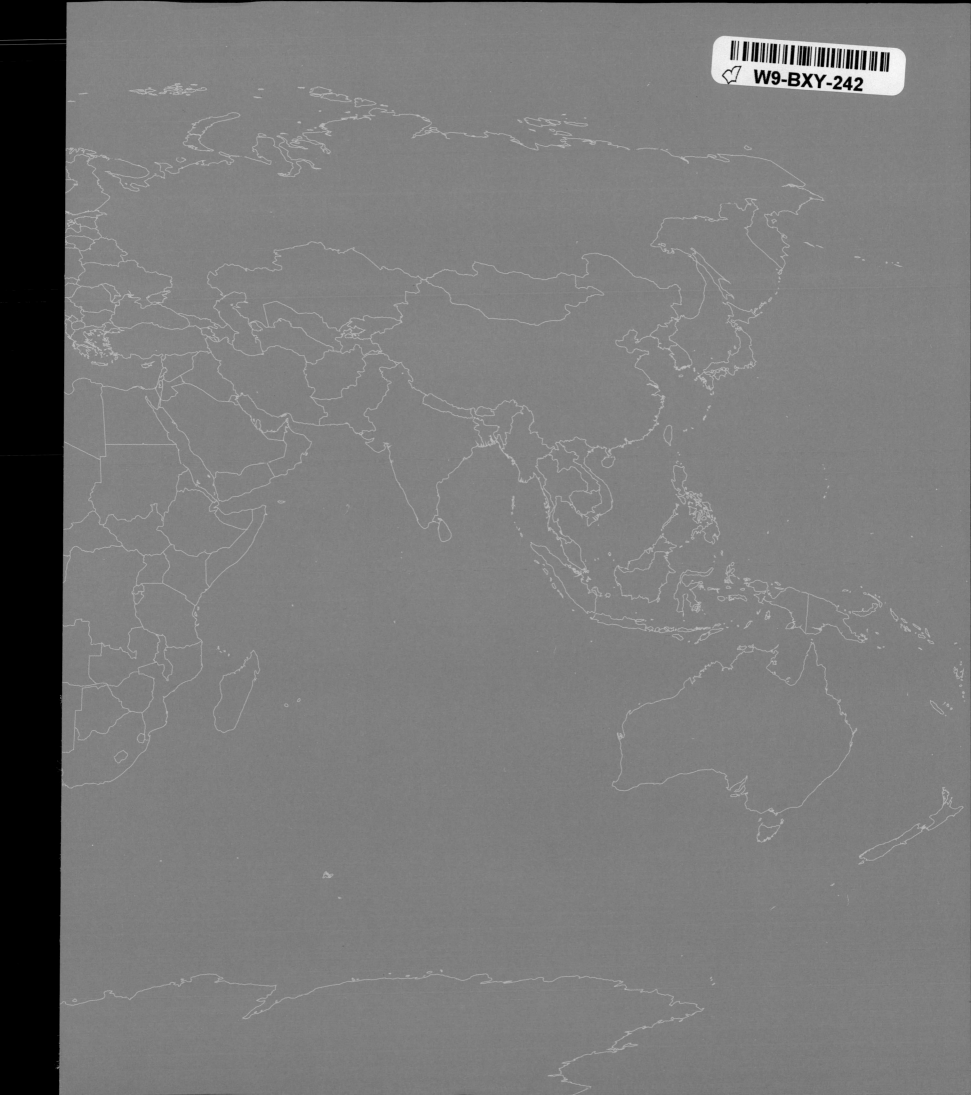

Globalography

First published in 2018 by White Lion Publishing,
an imprint of The Quarto Group.
The Old Brewery, 6 Blundell Street,
London, N7 9BH,
United Kingdom
T (0)20 7700 6700
www.QuartoKnows.com

A catalogue record for this book is available from the British Library.

ISBN 978 1 78131 791 4
Ebook ISBN 978 1 78131 871 3
Printed in Malaysia
10 9 8 7 6 5 4 3 2 1

Designed by Paileen Currie
Maps by Sam Vickars

Globalography

Our interconnected world revealed in 50 maps

CHRIS FITCH

Maps by Sam Vickars

WHITE LION PUBLISHING

Contents

Introduction

Imagine a standard world map, but with all the national borders and other man-made boundaries removed. In their place, visualize the constant flow of people, resources, money, data, ideas and commodities around the planet. Trace the strong connections that transcend borders, all interlinked and interdependent, with decisions and actions taken on one side of the planet having the most dramatic impact thousands of miles away – just like the metaphorical wings of a butterfly. This is our modern, globalized world.

It's easy to think that globalization is all about transnational corporations, free trade and capital flows. Undoubtedly, yes, money does make the world go round to some degree, but what about the lives of the actual people who are becoming increasingly globalized? How do they move around the world? What about the peripatetic exchange of culture, sport, architecture, art, technology and more? What about, even, the way the 'Gaia' principle shows the natural world to be highly globalized itself, as exhibited by the powerful currents that connect the world's oceans?

Globalization itself is no new phenomenon. But there is little doubt that the pace of change, and the modern, turbo-charged version of globalization we have seen unfolding in the early twenty-first century, has taken this idea to a new level of intensity. International tourists, financial transactions, energy reserves, military forces, raw materials, digital data. . . all these and many more can now travel across borders, covering thousands of miles, with the click of a mouse. The transnational status of many corporations and the global rich means they can exist nomadically, relocating and outsourcing as they please.

Consequentially, there has never been greater inequality than there is today, with just a handful of multi-billionaires holding as much wealth as half the global population. Furthermore, the more globalization takes place, the more the environment suffers, with plastic pollution, deforestation, species extinction, resource depletion and climate change all inevitable consequences of the extreme consumption that globalization aids and abets. On the other hand, the economic growth caused by globalization has helped global poverty rates plummet, from 42 per cent in 1981 to just 11 per cent by 2013. Similarly, average life expectancy has jumped, from just fifty-three years in 1960, to seventy-two by 2016.

It's therefore an opportune moment to explore individual examples that reveal how this new globalized world really operates. For example, entrepreneurs and manufacturers in one country can now find customers on the other side of the globe, while food products such as bananas, tea and cocoa can be bought by people thousands of miles from the climates where they are grown. Millions of young people are now free to travel abroad for their education, and enjoy the many opportunities that presents. Nations can donate their soldiers to become vital UN peacekeepers in some of the world's most troubled regions. Perhaps most dramatically, smartphones and online messaging have brought cheap and efficient communication to the world.

To help put all this into perspective, here we map fifty stories that reveal the myriad ways in which we now connect with one another. Some are perhaps to be expected, while others may take you by surprise. Together, they showcase the radical way globalization is transforming our world.

Bananas

The world's leading banana exporters, sized by total export value.

10k   100k   1m   10m   100m 1b   3b

US$

Bananas

In 1830, Joseph Paxton, head gardener at Chatsworth House in England's Peak District, found himself in possession of an unusual fruit that had been imported from Mauritius. He eventually managed to cultivate the plant in the stately home's greenhouse, and named it *Musa cavendishii* after his employers, the Cavendish family. Unbeknownst to either Paxton or the Cavendish family, this humble fruit would one day go on to take over the world.

Worldwide, over 100 billion bananas are consumed every single year. The world's favourite fruit – both nutritious and extremely conveniently 'packaged' – may arguably be the most unglamorous. But this commodity is the epitome of the modern global economy, with 17 million tonnes of bananas imported globally in 2016. Only rice, wheat and corn are more important crops in humanity's collective diet.

By far and away the world's largest exporter of bananas is currently Ecuador, selling $2.7 billion's worth in 2016, nearly one-quarter of all exported bananas, and far in excess of Guatemala, Costa Rica, Colombia, the Philippines or any other competitor. Deep, well-drained soils in humid tropical climates make optimum banana-growing conditions, which, combined with significant government support for the industry, has propelled the Ecuadorians to the top of the global production league.

The destinations to which the millions of bananas are exported by Ecuador and their tropical rivals are predictably the economic powerhouses of the European Union and the United States, who, together, import nearly 60 per cent of all bananas.

Thanks to the efforts of Paxton, and the missionaries who first transported the crop around the world, nearly half of all bananas grown globally are now of the Cavendish variety, totalling over 55 million tonnes. Crucially, almost the entirety of exported bananas are Cavendishes. In much of the rest of the world, where domestic demand is more important than the preferences of

Northern America
4.5
Europe
408.2
Oceania
1,641.9
Central America
9,721.5
South America
16,782.5
Africa
21,019.3
Asia
61,584.0

Despite the not insignificant size of operations in both Africa and South America, Asia is the undisputed leader in banana production. Figures are shown in 1,000 metric tons.

distant consumers, a far wider variety of bananas are grown and consumed (Ecuador reportedly has more than 300 different varieties).

However, the domination of the Cavendish banana may be coming to an end. The quirky reproduction method used in banana cultivation means that each Cavendish banana is a direct descendent – essentially a clone – of that first banana plant cultivated at Chatsworth House. This unusual biological heritage makes it almost impossible for the plants to develop the resistance to disease that comes from wide genetic variation, leaving them vulnerable. This is proving to be a particular problem as the world's Cavendish stock continues a relentless battle against the latest strain of Panama disease, a form of the fungus Fusarium wilt, which once wiped out the previous market leader, the Gros Michel banana, half a century ago. What could one day be a minor inconvenience to Western supermarket shoppers could be a serious economic headache for the world's major banana-producing countries. Might consumer tastes change sufficiently to enable Ecuador and fellow producers to start exporting different varieties of banana instead of Cavendishes? Or could the entire banana industry be on course to lose its global dominance?

Tourism: Most Visited Cities

The number of international overnight visitors in the most popular city destinations worldwide.

6.1   19.4

Million visitors

Tourism: Highest Spending

The leading cities in international visitor
spending worldwide.

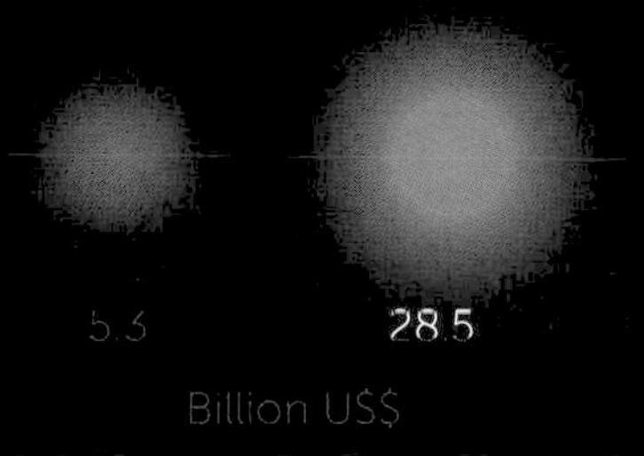

5.3   28.5

Billion US$

Tourism

There is one global industry that fails to have its growth dented: tourism. People have an apparently unrelenting desire for international travel. This should be no surprise, since studies have shown that regular travellers have a better sense of well-being and a more positive attitude towards life. One in ten jobs is now connected to tourism, and the past twenty years have seen a rapid rise in international tourists annually, from 563 million in 1996, to 1.2 billion by 2016, with forecasts predicting there will be as many as 1.8 billion by 2030.

The top destination for this wanderlust is Europe, with over 616 million tourists touching down in 2016, their itineraries taking them to see internationally recognized sites and to experience the architecture of Barcelona, the fashion-rich high streets of Milan and the canals of Amsterdam. The Asia-Pacific region is the next most popular, with over 308 million arrivals in 2016, which was more than double the number from ten years earlier, followed by North America at 130 million.

One significant observation is the key role of major cities as entry points to entire countries or regions. The world's most visited city is now Bangkok, with 19.41 million visitors in 2016. While the city's many fascinating and historic sites are no doubt attractive draws, just as important is the role the city plays as an entry point to South East Asia for visitors from Europe, the Americas and China. The next most visited cities play a similar 'hub' role in their respective continents, with London (19.06 million visitors) and Paris (15.45 million) serving as bases for tourists visiting Europe. Dubai (14.87 million) acts as a welcome to the Middle East, Istanbul (9.2 million) provides a literal and metaphorical bridge between Europe and Asia, while New York (12.7 million), that icon-filled melting pot of America, fulfils its other role as the grand entrance way to the United States. In this way, many global cities successfully take centre stage over and above their host countries.

London
19.06

Paris
15.45

Dubai
14.87

Bangkok
19.41

Singapore
13.11

Perhaps the most significant bucking of that trend is France, the most visited country in the entire world, with over 82 million visitors in 2016, followed by the United States and Spain, each with roughly 75 million visitors. Enjoying a central location in Western Europe, with famous vineyards and award-winning restaurants in every region, and a mix of Mediterranean beaches, Alpine mountains and historic towns, France is deservedly a popular country destination besides simply a visit to Paris.

There is also a ripple of change happening across international tourism, seeing countries such as China and Mexico hosting more tourists than ever before, with 59 million and 35 million tourists arriving each year respectively. Interestingly, rising incomes also mean that growing numbers of these populations are starting to travel themselves. Less than 35 million Chinese tourists travelled internationally in 2006, while over 135 million did so in 2016. Like never before, the world is on the move.

The 5 most visited cities, by millions of visitors in a year. The golden temples of Bangkok just pip the grand historical monuments of London to be the world's most visited city.

Peacekeepers

United Nations peacekeeper contribution, by country.
Inclusive of police, UN military experts on mission,
staff officers and troops.

0   1   10   100   1000   10,000
Number of personnel

15,000
5,000
100

Sized by deployed personnel on current operations

Peacekeepers

March 2018 saw the end of a fifteen-year UN peace-keeping mission to the West African nation of Liberia, codenamed UNMIL. The mission first started in 2003, following the overthrow of President Charles Taylor after years of civil war. Thanks to the efforts of 126,000 military personnel, 16,000 police officers and 23,000 civilian staff, stability slowly returned to the country. After three peaceful democratic elections, the decision was made to declare the mission a success, and bring it to a close.

UN peacekeepers are drawn from a vast array of contributing nations, with more than 120 members of the United Nations contributing at least someone to the force. In Liberia, they included people from regional neighbours such as Nigeria and Ghana, but also from countries far away, such as Pakistan and the Philippines. This wild mixing of nationalities in the interest of world peace is a perfectly ordinary situation in the world of UN peacekeepers and the network of more than 110,000 personnel known as the 'Blue Helmets', after their distinctive headwear. As employees of their own national militaries, soldiers and police officers from around the world can opt to spend a year, or perhaps two, on assignment with the UN, providing vital stability in those regions of the world where the risk of conflict remains a substantial threat.

Crucially, a peacekeeper's income during his or her service with the UN is paid by the organisation. For peacekeepers from developing nations, this is often significantly more than their standard domestic pay. This financial benefit is, perhaps, one reason why UN peacekeepers tend to originate overwhelmingly from countries such as Ethiopia (8,338), Bangladesh (7,023) and Rwanda (6,815), the three highest contributors in early 2018. Southeast Asia and southern Africa were also heavily represented, while major militaristic nations such as France and the United Kingdom contributed 820 and 659 respectively.

Seventy years on from the founding of the United Nations, its peacekeeping force remains overwhelmingly male, with women only making up a few thousand of the total force. The UN certainly aims to increase the number of women actively involved in peacekeeping, since an authoritative female presence can have a major impact on improving community attitudes towards women in many of the conflict-afflicted regions in which the UN operates.

A total of seventy-one missions have been launched since the UN first set up UNTSO to intervene in Palestine in May 1948, the very first such mission. Having never been concluded, UNTSO is also the longest-running mission, and joins other similar involvements such as that between India and Pakistan (UNMOGIP, since January 1949) and in divided Cyprus (UNFICYP, since March 1964). The end of the Liberia mission left fourteen active UN peacekeeping missions across the globe. Half of them are in Africa, including in Mali (MINUSMA), Western Sahara (MINURSO), Darfur, Sudan (UNAMID) and the Central African Republic (MINUSCA). One mission is currently active in the Caribbean (Haiti, MINUJUSTH), one in Europe (Kosovo, UNMIK) and two in the Middle East (Lebanon, UNIFIL, and the Golan, UNDOF). Overall, more than one million people have served as UN peacekeepers over the past seventy years, with 3,500 people losing their lives in the line of duty.

Haiti (Port-au-Prince)
1202

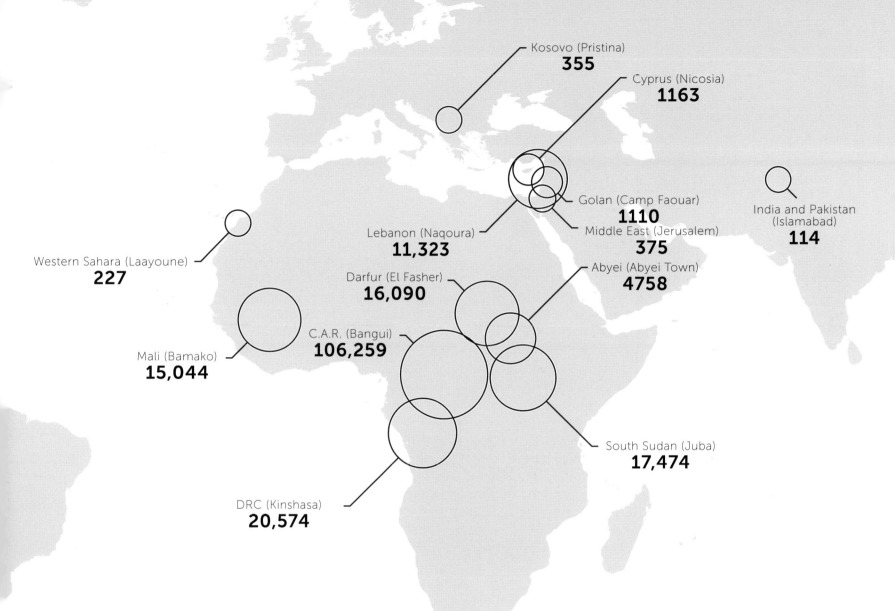

Kosovo (Pristina)
355

Cyprus (Nicosia)
1163

Golan (Camp Faouar)
1110

Middle East (Jerusalem)
375

Lebanon (Naqoura)
11,323

India and Pakistan
(Islamabad)
114

Western Sahara (Laayoune)
227

Darfur (El Fasher)
16,090

Abyei (Abyei Town)
4758

C.A.R. (Bangui)
106,259

Mali (Bamako)
15,044

South Sudan (Juba)
17,474

DRC (Kinshasa)
20,574

The number of
peacekeepers stationed
in the fourteen current UN
Peacekeeping operations,
the majority of which
are either in Africa or
the Middle East.

15,000

5,000

100 personnel

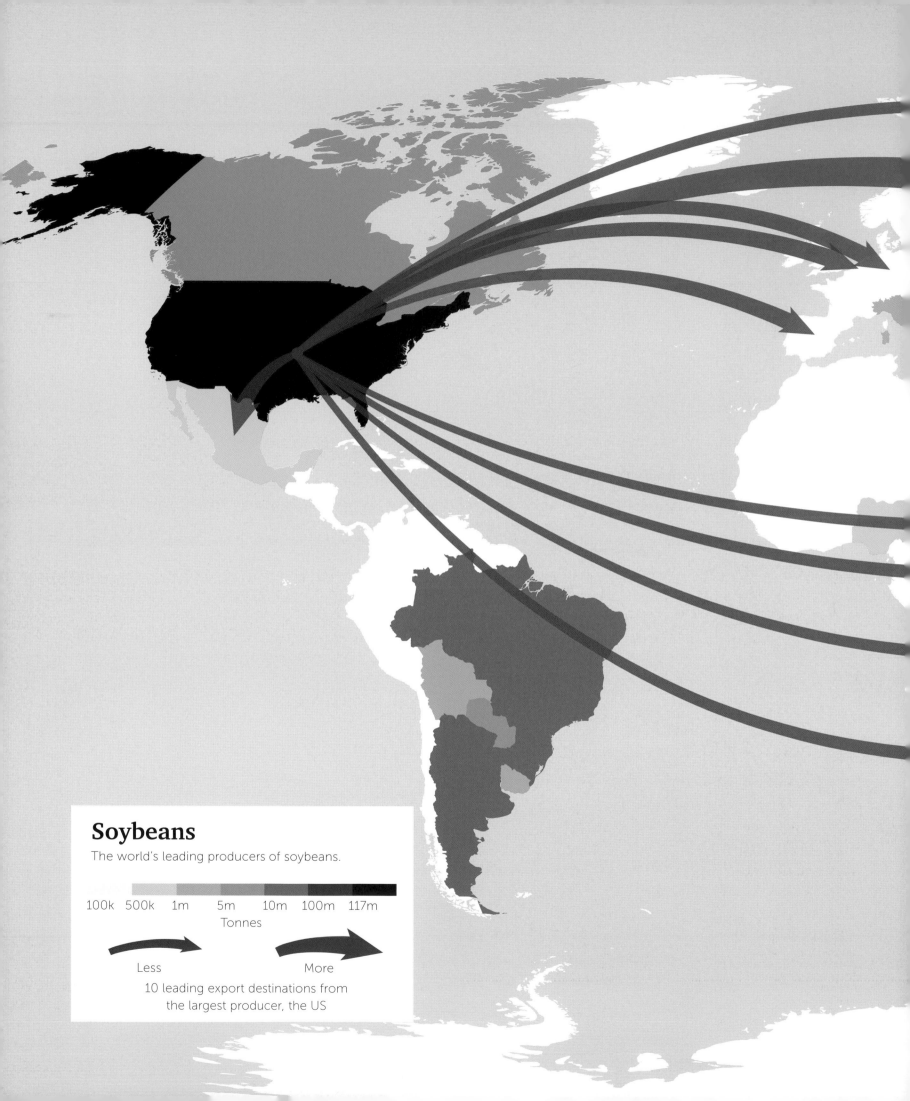

Soybeans

The world's leading producers of soybeans.

100k	500k	1m	5m	10m	100m	117m

Tonnes

Less   More

10 leading export destinations from
the largest producer, the US

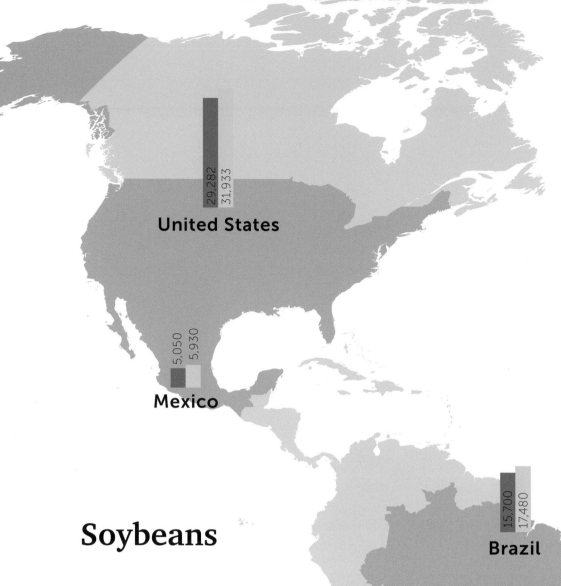

United States

29,282
31,933

5,050
5,930

Mexico

15,700
17,480

Brazil

Soybeans

The soybean is known for its versatility – as a protein-rich alternative to meat products, as an oil used in cakes, crackers and for packing tinned fish, and in all manner of non-edible products from candles and carpets to foams and fuels. Originating from East Asia, where it has been a staple of regular diets in China, Korea and Japan for millennia, the soybean was warmly welcomed into its adopted home, the United States of America, during the early years of the twentieth century. William J. Morse, a scientist at the US Department of Agriculture (USDA), is commonly known as the father of American soy, for his life's work researching thousands of strains of soybean before importing the crop and establishing a thriving industry in the US.

Morse had help. Henry Ford, the man known for turning the automobile into something that could be mass-produced cheaply enough for it to be owned by all, saw the potential in Morse's soybeans as a replacement for crops such as corn and wheat. The wide diversity of products that could be made using soy was highly appealing and Ford sold everything from baked goods to ice cream manufactured from soybeans. Almost a century on, the United States is the world's largest producer of soybeans, growing 121 million tonnes in 2017. The highest producing state is Illinois, producing nearly 600 million bushels (one bushel is 27.2kg/60lb), followed by Iowa (570 million) and Minnesota (400 million). Not far behind the Americans, the next-highest producer is Brazil, with 107 million tonnes, followed by Argentina, with 57 million, and much smaller quantities in China, India, Paraguay and Canada.

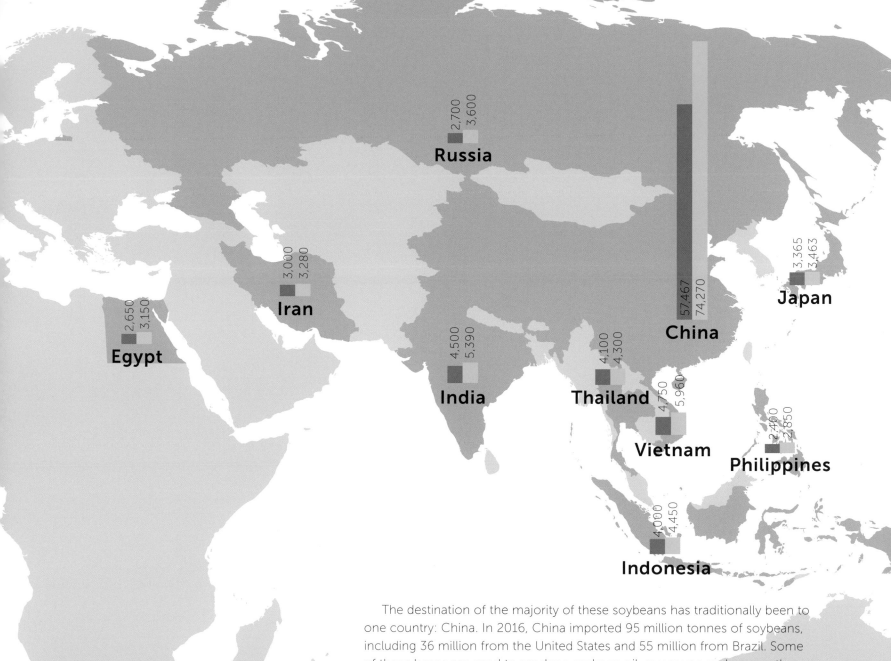

Russia
2,700
3,600

Iran
3,000
3,280

Egypt
2,650
3,150

India
4,500
5,390

Thailand
4,100
4,300

China
57,467
74,270

Japan
3,365
3,463

Vietnam
4,750
5,960

Philippines
2,400
2,850

Indonesia
4,000
4,450

The destination of the majority of these soybeans has traditionally been to one country: China. In 2016, China imported 95 million tonnes of soybeans, including 36 million from the United States and 55 million from Brazil. Some of these beans are used to produce soybean oil, soy sauce, and many other foodstuffs, but the majority are used to feed livestock – everything from chickens to pigs to cattle. The beans are a cheap source of protein to grow farm animals to a size where they can be slaughtered for a comfortable profit. So plentiful are soybeans in animal feed across the world, that the average human omnivore in the developed world indirectly consumes far more soy through their meat intake than people who directly consume soy products such as tofu or soy milk.

Unfortunately, the environmental impact of growing soybeans on an industrial scale is gradually revealing itself to be significantly damaging. One large problem has been the indiscriminate clearing of land in the Amazon rainforest to create vast plantations in order to keep up with the demand for feed. Currently soy comprises approximately 13 per cent of the crops grown on cleared Amazon land. Since the implementation of managed deforestation in 2008, such land use has fallen dramatically, from nearly 7,000 sq km (2,700 sq miles) annually prior to 2008, to a total of just 474 sq km (183 sq miles) in the ten years to 2018. Such practices could help eliminate the soybean's negative reputation, meaning the bean may yet regain that revolutionary aroma that so attracted Morse and Ford.

China are overwhelmingly the world's biggest consumers of soybeans, perhaps explained by the popularity of soy sauce and other soy-based food products.

2014–15
2017–18
Consumption, thousand tonnes

Tea

Tea consumption per capita.

0.03　　4.4　　1.28　　6.96
Pounds

5 leading tea producing countries, sized by
volume produced

Tea

Which country is the spiritual home of tea? Many cultures, including Britain, India and China may think that they hold this title. But there is nowhere in the world where tea comprises a more significant part of daily life than in Turkey. The average Turkish person will consume as much as 3.16kg (6.96lb) of tea annually – that's more than 1,500 cups of tea a year for every man, woman and child – substantially more than the citizens of any other country.

Prior to the twentieth century, tea was a relatively niche drink in Turkey, with coffee the cup of choice. All this was soon to change following the publication in 1878 of *Çay Risalesi* (*The Tea Pamphlet*), a popular book that preached the health benefits of tea. Combined with a change in prices that eventually saw several glasses of tea costing the same as a single coffee, a significant cultural shift was underway.

The town of Rize on the Black Sea coast, became the first domestic producer of Turkish tea in the early 1900s, with many others soon following suit. During the twentieth century, the word *çay*, Turkish for 'tea', was even incorporated into the new names of several towns who wished to become known for their tea production – Kadahor changed to Çaykara and Mapavri became Çayeli. Tea grown in the Black Sea region remains the most popular variety in Turkey today, and although apple, rosehip, sage and linden blossom are popular alternatives, traditional strong black tea reigns supreme. If there's one unacceptable faux pas in Turkey, it's being the host who runs out of tea. As a guest, the only way to stop your glass being topped up endlessly is to deliberately place a teaspoon atop the glass as soon as it becomes empty, a clear signal to your relieved host.

Following in Turkey's footsteps as the greatest consumers of tea are, perhaps predictably, the Irish and the British, at 2.19 and 1.94kg (4.83 and 4.28lb) per year respectively. The key difference between these countries and Turkey is that neither is capable of cultivating their own tea, both being dependent on importing significant quantities of (predominantly black) tea from such distant countries as Kenya, India and Malawi. However, the world's largest importers of tea are the Russians, followed by Pakistan, the United Arab Emirates and the United States, all of whom act as regional 'hubs', later re-exporting the tea to neighbouring countries.

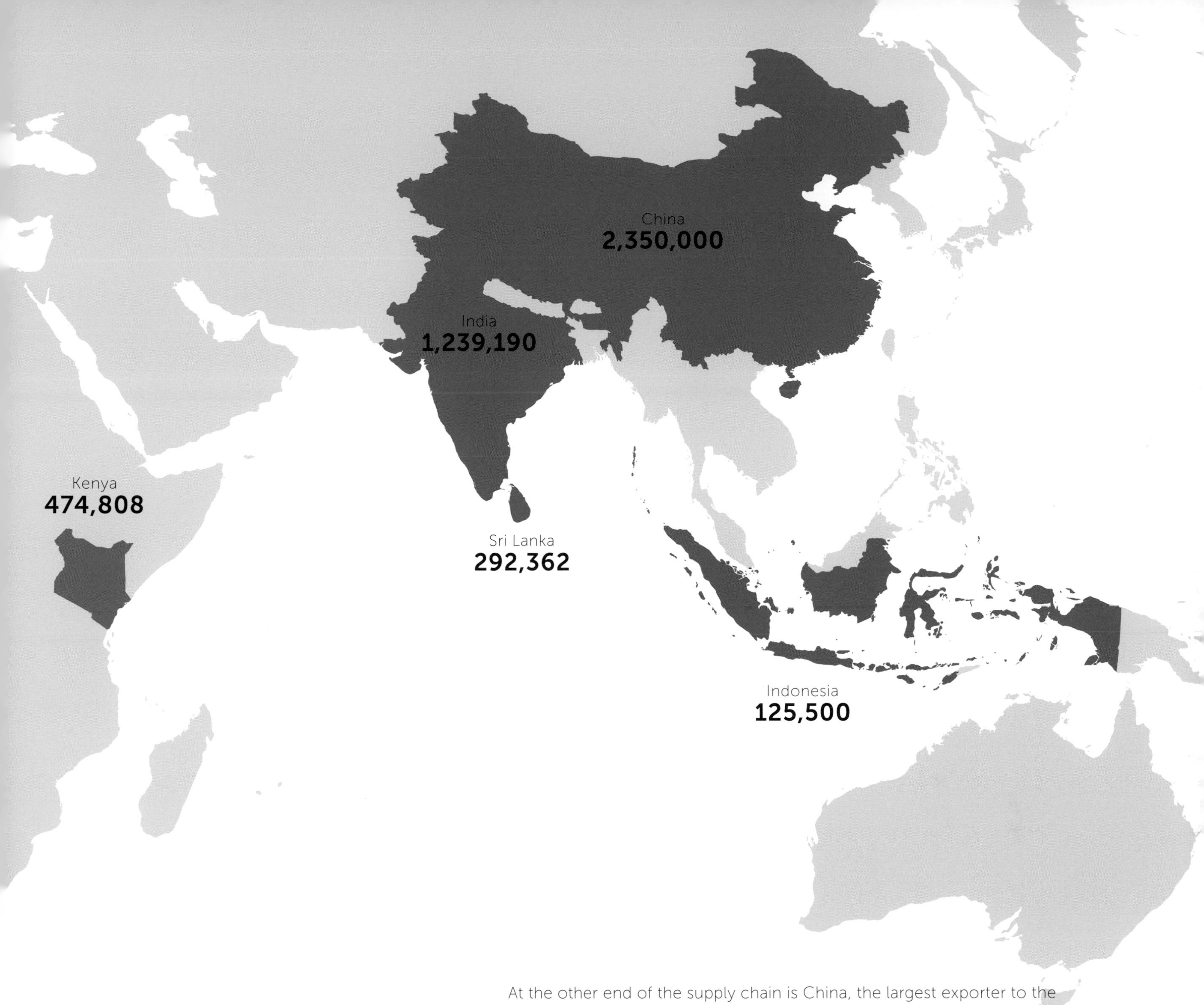

China
2,350,000

India
1,239,190

Kenya
474,808

Sri Lanka
292,362

Indonesia
125,500

While China and India overwhelmingly lead the world in tea production, rivals such as Sri Lanka and Kenya produce respectable quantities, given their smaller sizes. Figures in tonnes.

At the other end of the supply chain is China, the largest exporter to the rest of the world – selling 2.35 million tonnes of tea annually, worth nearly $1.5 billion – followed by India and Sri Lanka. Tea has been grown in China for millennia, with its seeds beginning to travel in the year 800, first to Japan, then around the world. After wealthy Europeans had become hooked on imported tea, the nineteenth century saw a significant expansion in plantations across India and Sri Lanka, promoted and controlled by British colonialists. Like Turkey, Sri Lanka only began mass-producing tea relatively recently, following a devastating blight in the 1860s and 1870s that almost wiped out the island's coffee plantations. Growers turned to tea, and the damp and cool mountain environment proved to be ideal conditions for what would later become Sri Lanka's distinctively unique variety of black tea.

These countries, along with Kenya, Indonesia, and many others, are the driving force behind a surge in global tea production from around 2.7 million tonnes back in 2006, to as much as 4.4 million tonnes just ten years later.

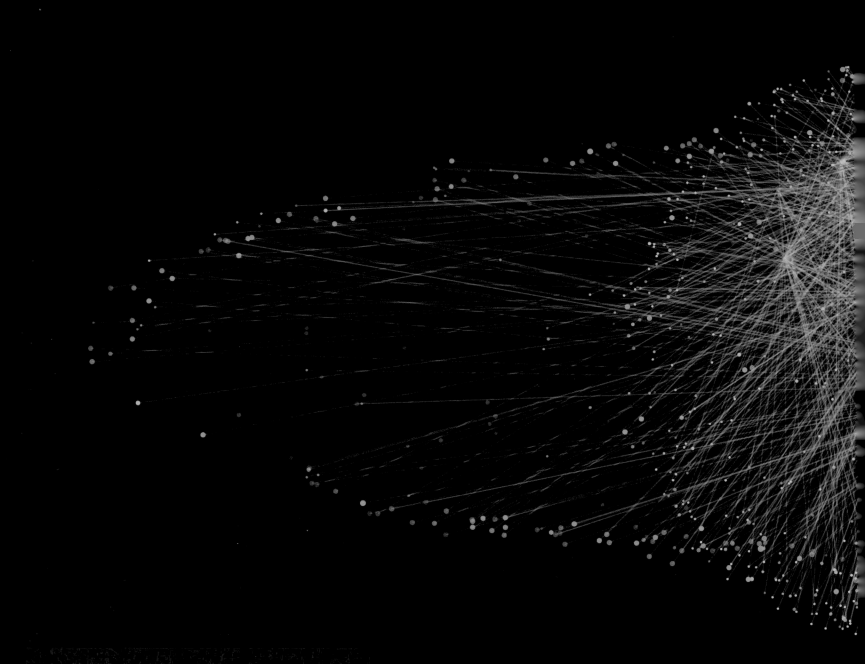

Satellites: Purpose and Life Expectancy

Satellite location — Launch site

Shorter · • ● Longer   Younger ● ● ● Older
Life expectancy   Age

- ● Communications
- ● Earth observation
- ○ Space observation
- ● Technology demonstration
- ● Navigation
- ● Earth science
- ○ Space science
- ● Technology department

Purpose

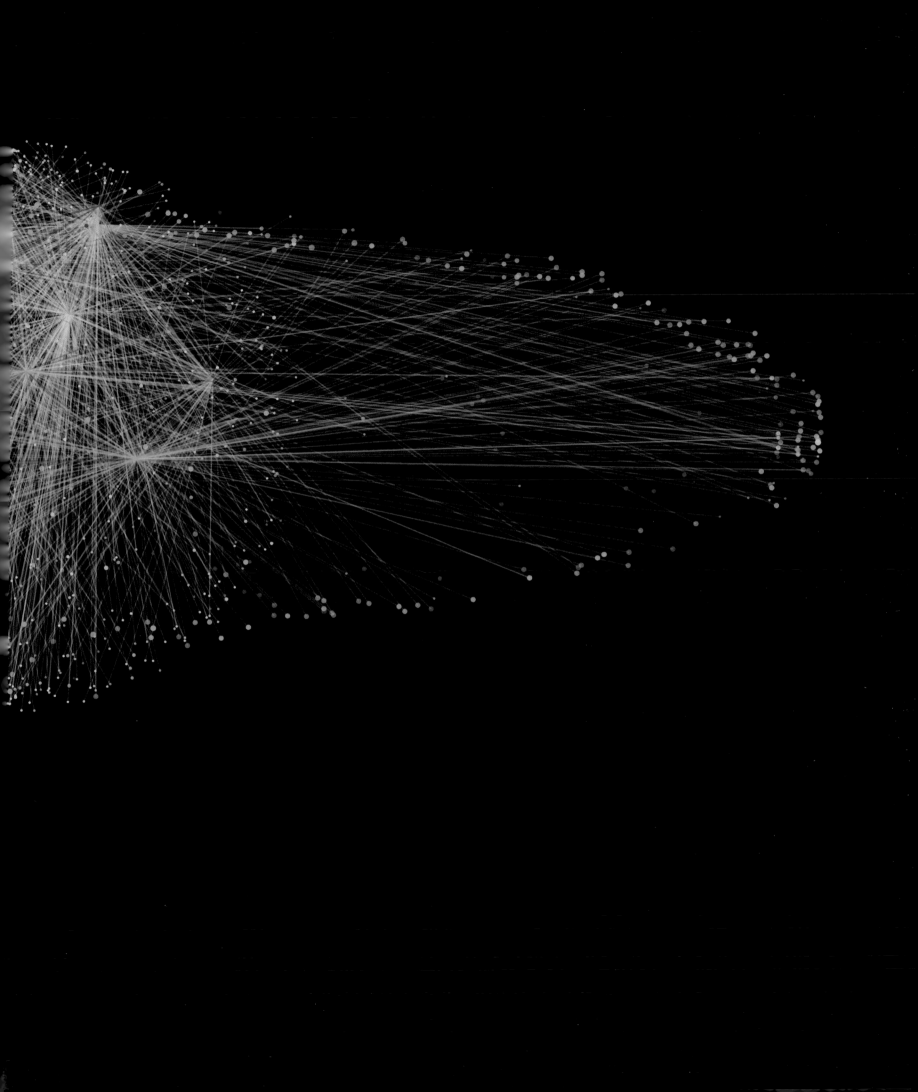

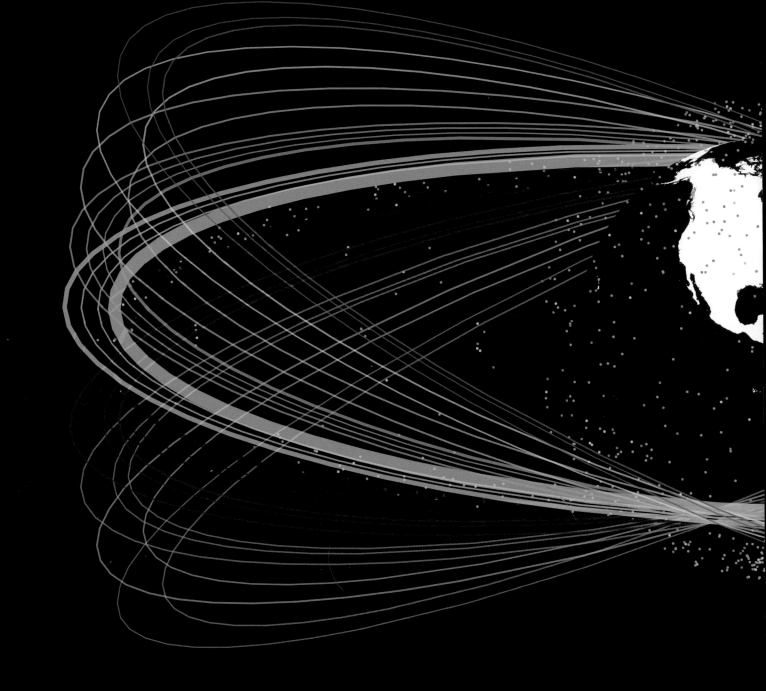

Satellites: Ownership and Operation

User

● Civil ● Commercial
● Government ● Military

France
Canada
India
Russia
United States
China
Japan
United Kingdom
European Space Agency
Germany

| 2 | 100 | 123 |

Number of satellites operated, by country

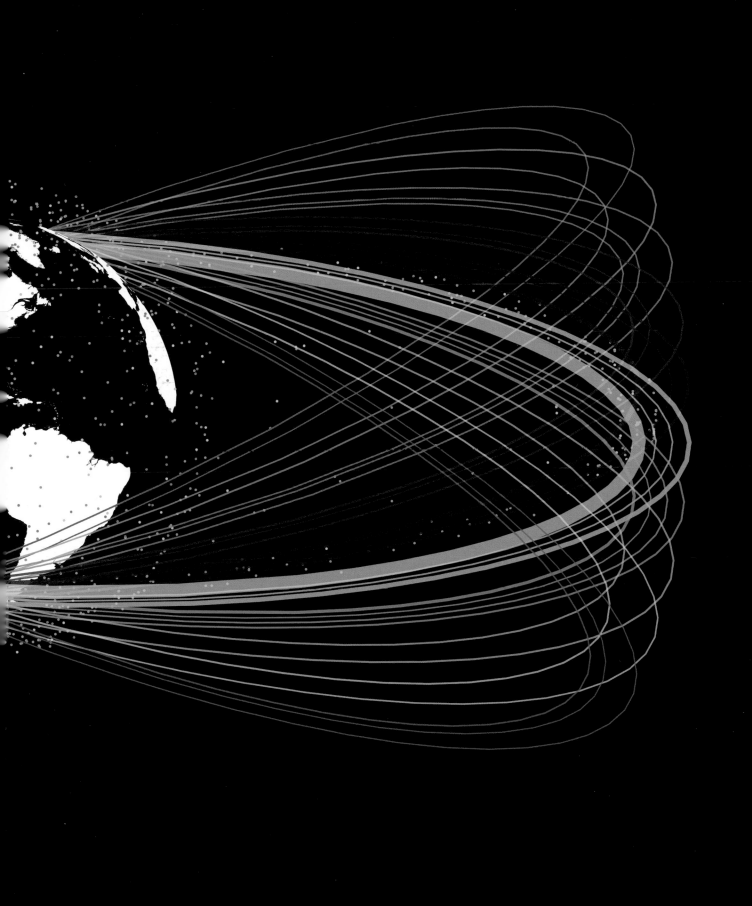

Satellites

In October 1957, a rocket blasted off from a remote launch site in modern-day Kazakhstan. It was carrying *Sputnik 1*, set to make history as the world's very first artificial satellite. By the mid-1960s, there were only a handful of countries with their own satellites in orbit; the United States, the United Kingdom, Canada, Russia, France and Italy. Since then, in excess of 6,600 artificial satellites have been launched, and as of August 2017, there are now 1,738 operational satellites orbiting the planet.

Today's active satellites include a mix of military, commercial and civil instruments, designed to perform beneficial actions back down on Earth for as many reasons as you could possibly imagine. There are satellites that enable mobile devices to connect to one another; satellites guiding vehicles around the world; and satellites constantly taking photographs of the Earth's surface.

The world's largest launcher of satellites is the United States, with 803 currently in orbit, followed by China, with 204, and Russia, with 142. While 150 of the American satellites are owned by the US government, and 159 are for military purposes, the majority (476) are owned and operated by commercial entities. Whereas launching a satellite used to mean spending upwards of tens of thousands of dollars in order to send large objects into orbit, the creation of the very small and light 'CubeSat' means most satellite operations can now be performed by a gadget you could hold in your hand. Costs have plummeted as a result, and business is booming.

Once ejected from the Earth's atmosphere a satellite can be programmed to follow the unique requirements of each device. There are three main orbit levels into which satellites are launched. The further a satellite is from the surface, the weaker the force of gravity, and therefore the longer it takes to complete a full rotation of the planet. A distance of 180–2,000km (112–1,240 miles) from the Earth's surface is the low Earth orbit (LEO), where most scientific satellites can be found. The biggest artificial satellite ever launched remains the International Space Station (ISS), which, at between 347–360km (215–225 miles) above the Earth, is in a LEO, where it completes a full circuit every ninety-one minutes. Crew upon the ISS witness an extraordinary sunrise every one-and-a-half hours, completing nearly sixteen full circuits of the planet every single day. Medium Earth orbit (MEO), between 2,000–36,000km (1,240–22,400 miles) from the surface, is where most navigation satellites can be found.

Furthest from the Earth, high Earth orbit (HEO), is anywhere above 36,000km (22,400 miles). This is where satellites designed to rotate exactly in sync with the planet are located, focusing on one specific spot on the Earth's surface. These are particularly useful for weather-monitoring and communication satellites, which take close to twenty-four hours to complete a circuit.

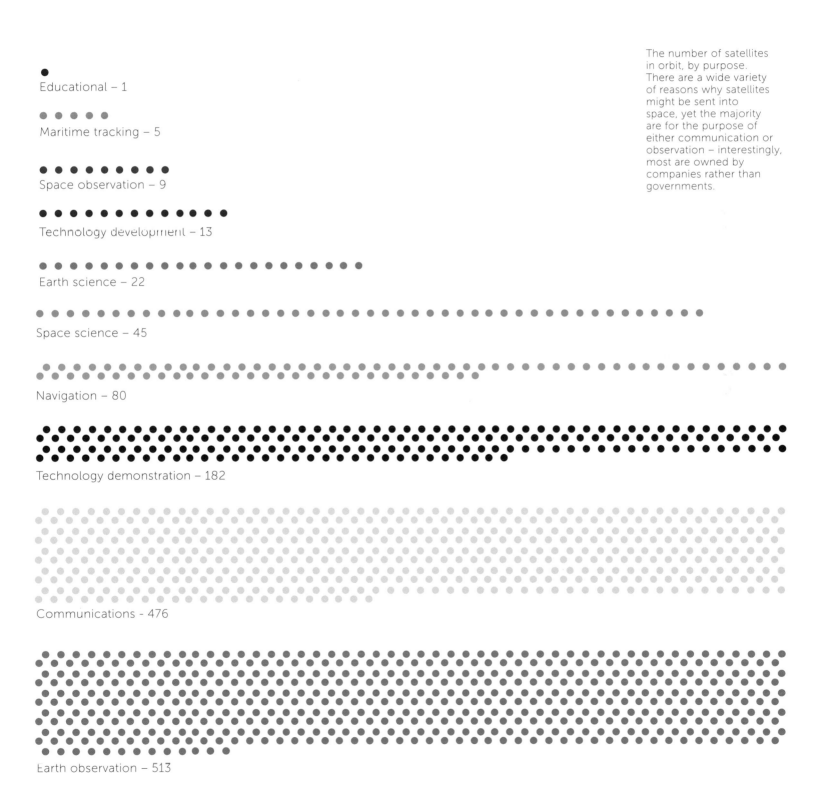

Educational – 1

Maritime tracking – 5

Space observation – 9

Technology development – 13

Earth science – 22

Space science – 45

Navigation – 80

Technology demonstration – 182

Communications - 476

Earth observation – 513

The number of satellites in orbit, by purpose. There are a wide variety of reasons why satellites might be sent into space, yet the majority are for the purpose of either communication or observation – interestingly, most are owned by companies rather than governments.

Uranium

The world's leading consumers of uranium.

0.36   18.69

Kilotons

Less   More

Uranium imported by the largest consumer, the US.

Belgium
9.8

Canada
23.2

UK
16.2

France
91.2

United States
191.8

Spain
13.3

Uranium

The modern unit of currency, the 'dollar', has its origins in the word 'thaler'. It's a shortening of 'Joachimsthaler', the name for a specific type of coin minted from silver obtained from mines in a town called Joachimsthal, now Jáchymov in modern day Czech Republic. It was from these mines that professional apothecary, accomplished businessman and intrigued eighteenth-century scientist Martin Heinrich Klaproth found himself studying material known colloquially as 'pitchblende'. This dark and mysterious substance was a byproduct of the silver-mining process, and nobody had yet worked out exactly what it was. Klaproth was the first to identify the unique material contained within it, in 1789, and he named it 'uranium' after the planet Uranus, which had been discovered just eight years earlier.

Klaproth could never have guessed it at the time, but uranium went on to play a major role in shaping the twentieth century, with the process of nuclear fission – the dividing of an atom's nucleus, which releases a huge amount of energy – enabling everything from the horrifying destruction wrought upon Hiroshima and Nagasaki in 1945 and the decades of tense geopolitical standoffs that ensued, to the mainstream development of domestic nuclear energy and the disastrous scenes observed at Chernobyl and Fukushima. None of this would have been possible without uranium-235, a naturally occurring but rare form of uranium (only around 0.7 per cent of global reserves), from which industrial nuclear activity is derived. When uranium ore samples are mined out of the ground, they are composed almost entirely (more than 99 per cent) of uranium-238. The extracted uranium metal needs to be enriched – reducing the number of neutrons inside uranium-238 atoms, thereby converting them to uranium-235 – in order to be radioactive enough

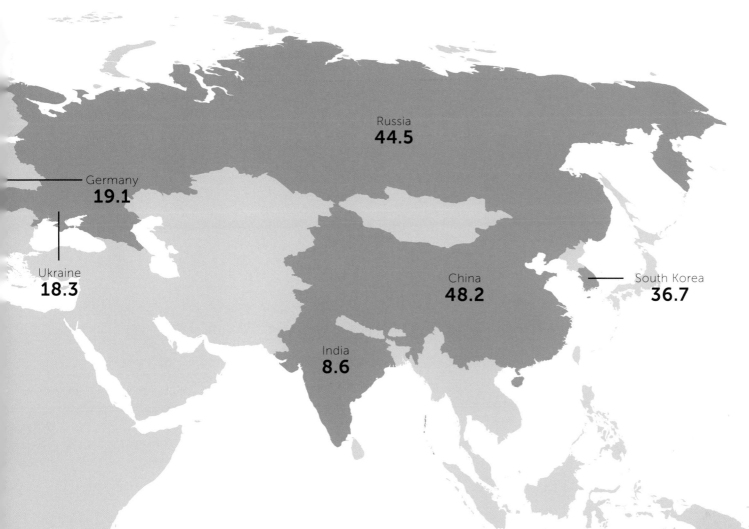

Russia
44.5

Germany
19.1

Ukraine
18.3

China
48.2

South Korea
36.7

India
8.6

for nuclear fission. Above around 5 per cent is considered suitably enriched, while the remaining low radioactive uranium-238 is considered 'depleted'.

Natural uranium is a highly plentiful element – at least as common as tin and about forty times more so than silver. Several countries have vast uranium reserves, and consequently large uranium exports. While one-third of the world's known uranium reserves are in Australia, significant quantities are also found in Kazakhstan, Russia and Canada. The world's two largest uranium mines – McArthur River and Cigar Lake – are both in Canada, yet the world's biggest uranium producer is currently Kazakhstan, with around 24,500 tonnes annually (compared to 14,000 for Canada and 6,300 for Australia).

Canada and Kazakhstan are therefore the biggest exporters to easily the world's largest importer of uranium, the United States, whose ninety-nine operable nuclear reactors consumed 18,000 tonnes of the element in 2016. The next highest importers are France, Russia, China and South Korea, all countries whose national grids are composed of above-average sources of nuclear power. Sales of uranium are restricted to countries that have signed the 1968 Treaty on the Non-Proliferation of Nuclear Weapons. The intention is to prevent the spread of nuclear weapons and weapons technology, while simultaneously allowing countries to develop nuclear power stations. However the extreme difficulties in enriching enough uranium to get the quantities of uranium-235 necessary for nuclear fission means there are long-term limits to its usefulness, with global supplies likely to be exhausted within the next century if current consumption rates continue.

Leading countries in nuclear energy consumption, in million tonnes of oil equivalent. The United States is comfortably the world's largest consumer.

Football Players

National soccer teams at the 2018 World Cup, by share of players at foreign clubs.

0%   75% 100%

Football Players

Could this be the secret to trophy success? For passionate supporters of football, the world's most popular sport, there is no end to the statistics and factors that can be pored over – from training rituals to wage structures – to try to find what makes a winning team. But does the success of a national football team depend in any way on whether their players play regular club football in their own domestic league, or whether they choose to move to another country to test themselves in a different league?

Only two 2018 FIFA World Cup-qualifying teams, Sweden and Senegal – not exactly the most trophy-laden of nations – have all of their national players playing overseas. While the Swedish Allsvenskan and the Senegal Premier League do exist, their relatively meagre wages and lack of top talent mean that any world class players that emerge are likely to be bought by a big European team the moment they show their potential. Belgium, Iceland, Switzerland and Nigeria all find themselves in a similar situation, each having only one player in their squads playing in their respective domestic leagues.

At the other extreme, countries such as Russia – winners of the 1960 European Championship – and Saudi Arabia – three times winners of the Asian Cup – have almost all of their footballers playing in their domestic league. England, winners of a solitary World Cup in 1966, is the only country whose national team is dominated by 'domestic' players, largely thanks to the wealth and consequentially market-warping forces of the English Premier League which attracts star players.

The wealth of the English leagues also gives them the distinction of having significantly more overseas players than any other, with an overwhelming 69 per cent of Premier League players coming from outside England. The next nearest is the Cypriot First Division, with 57 per cent, while the next top league is the Italian Serie A, where 56 per cent are ineligible for the Italian national team. Even the English Championship – the second division in England – and the Scottish Premiership both have a roughly 50–50 split between domestic and foreign players, among the highest in all of Europe.

Perhaps the recipe for international trophy success lies somewhere in the middle, by having a mix of players based in either a strong domestic league or within lucrative leagues overseas. Two of the most successful European nations, Germany and Spain, have around one-third of their players employed in many of the best-performing teams overseas, with the other two-thirds playing in their top-ranking domestic leagues. Equally, the most successful non-European nations are the South American giants of Brazil and Argentina. Both of these two combine having around 80 per cent of their players based overseas – almost entirely in the top teams in Europe – with competitive and relatively high-quality domestic leagues (the Brazilian Série A and Argentine Primera Division). Perhaps this balance is the real key to trophy success.

Sweden

England

Senegal

100%

0%

England is the only World Cup team to have their entire squad playing for domestic clubs, while neither Senegal nor Sweden have any players who are based at home.

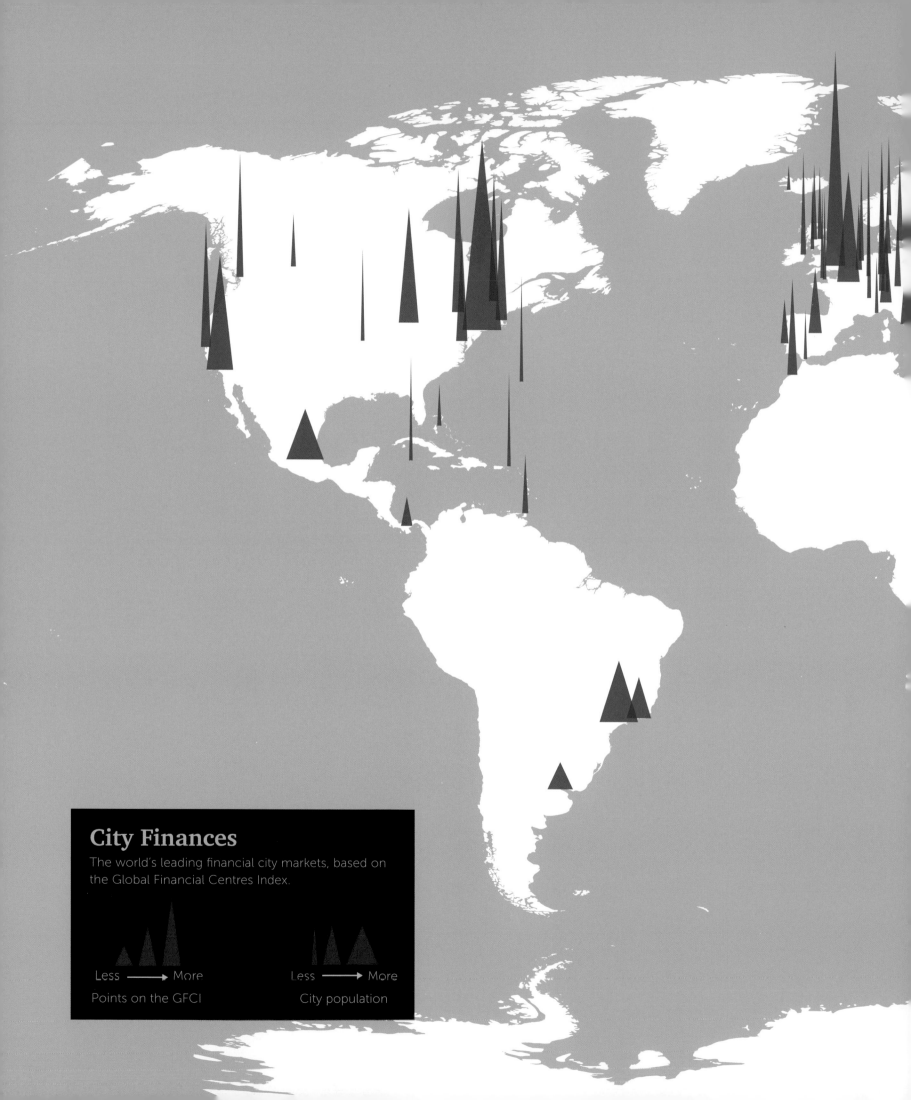

City Finances

The world's leading financial city markets, based on the Global Financial Centres Index.

Less ⟶ More
Points on the GFCI

Less ⟶ More
City population

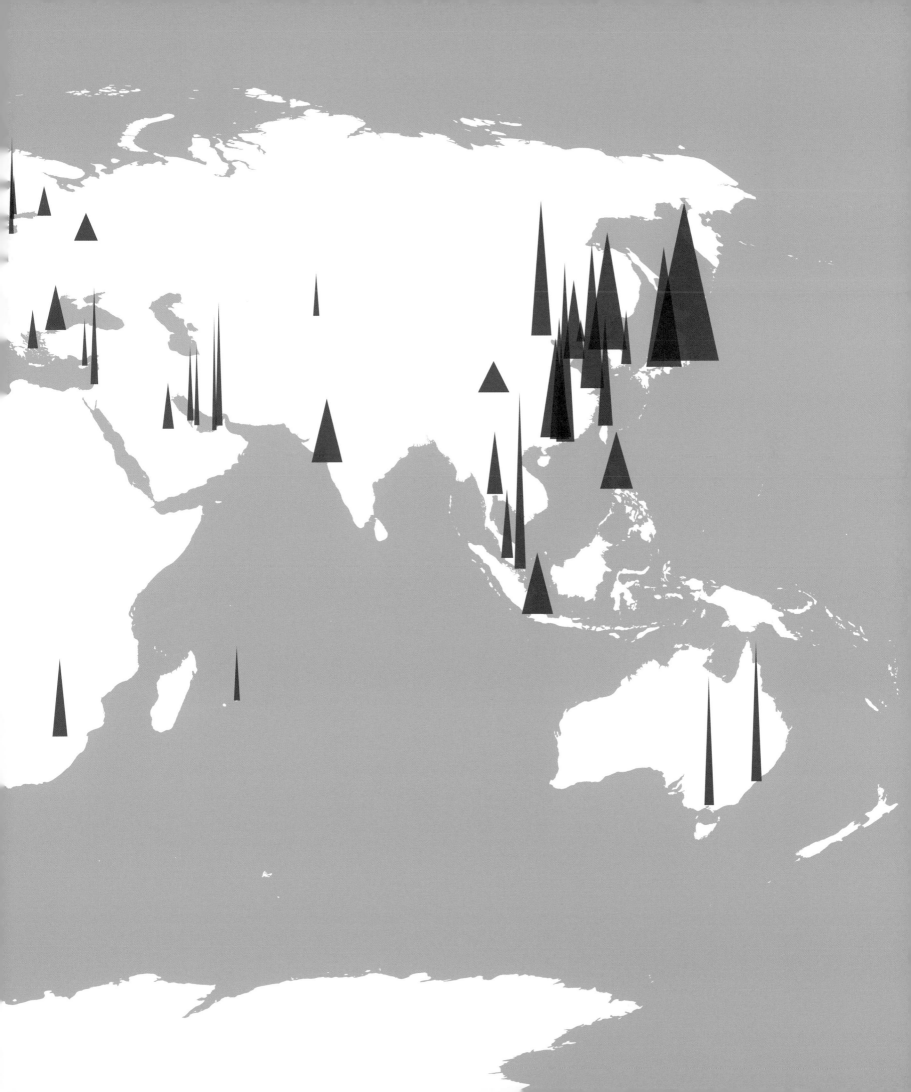

London
780

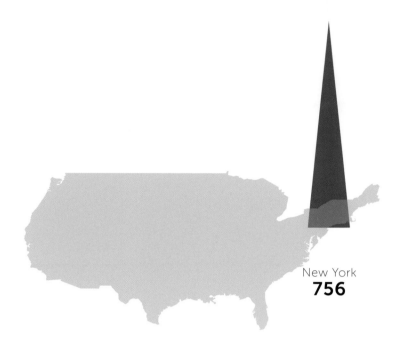

New York
756

City Finances

London is 5,600km (3,500 miles) from New York, which in turn is 12,900km (8,000 miles) from Hong Kong. But these vast distances, so important for centuries, when commercial trade and human migration established them as key urban hubs, mean almost nothing today. At least, not in the new world of high finance, where cities are connected by computers that make trades in fractions of seconds in response to events occurring on the other side of the world.

According to the Global Financial Centres Index (GFCI) – a ranking of 110 of the world's financial centres based on a mix of factors including the availability of skilled employees, political stability and the quality of infrastructure – London, New York and Hong Kong are currently the three most powerful financial cities in the world. All three have an English-speaking population, strong reputations as long-term successful business centres and close connections to regional neighbours. The importance of Asia's booming urban economies is shown by the presence of Singapore, Tokyo and Shanghai as the next three cities on this list, followed by Toronto, Sydney, Zurich and Beijing.

By far the biggest financial trading machines in the world can be found in the United States – specifically New York, where the NASDAQ and New York Stock Exchange (NYSE) get cosy with their investments and assets on iconic Broadway and Wall Street respectively. Behind the United States, China is home to the Shanghai and Shenzen-ChiNext stock exchanges, which have grown rapidly since their launches in the early 1990s, threatening to steal a march on Hong Kong, the country's traditional financial hub.

A number of cities, such as Shanghai and Tokyo, have become major financial hubs by virtue of their large populations. Others thrive because finance is their key business activity. This is especially the case in central Europe. The Swiss cities of Zurich (population 1.2 million) and Geneva (200,000) rank as the ninth and fifteenth biggest financial centres in the world. Tiny Luxembourg City sits fourteenth on the list, despite a total population of only 114,000 people (out of 594,000 people in the whole of Luxembourg), particularly thanks to strong cross-border connections with the rest of Europe, and generous tax giveaways to incentivise corporations to relocate. During the second half of the twentieth century, the economy of Luxembourg transformed from one focused on steel manufacturing, to one that revolves entirely around private banking, insurance and corporate lending in this relatively small urban hub; currently Luxembourg's financial sector accounts for in excess of 35 per cent of national GDP. The economic clout of Luxembourg City allows the country as a whole to punch above its weight on the international stage, alongside such heavyweights as London, New York and Hong Kong.

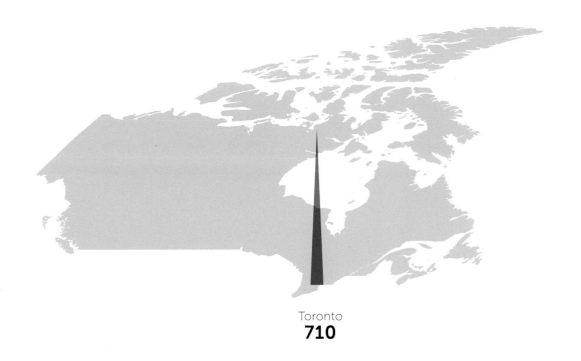

Toronto
710

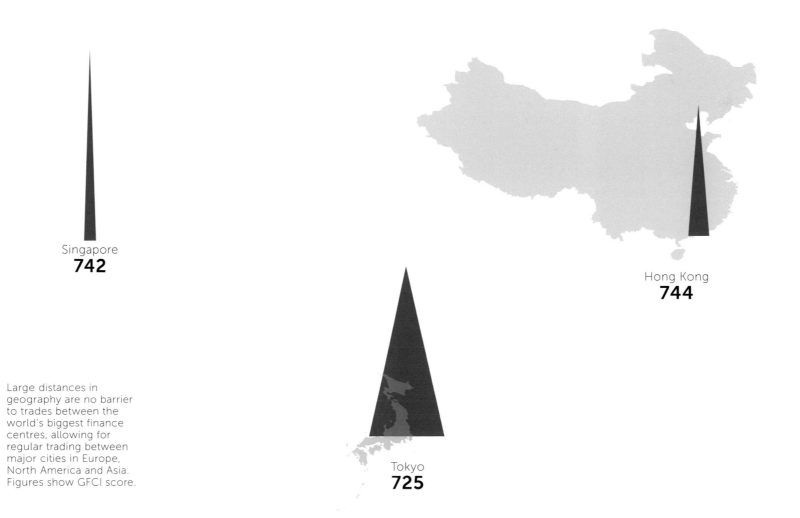

Singapore
742

Hong Kong
744

Large distances in geography are no barrier to trades between the world's biggest finance centres, allowing for regular trading between major cities in Europe, North America and Asia. Figures show GFCI score.

Tokyo
725

Palm Oil

The leading countries in domestic consumption
of palm oil.

800k   11m
Tonnes

Palm Oil

Biscuits. Cereal. Ice cream. Soap. It may be surprising to learn that the everyday foods and household commodities in this list share a common ingredient: palm oil. In fact, the sheer number of products in which palm oil is a major ingredient is staggering, especially considering how rapidly this particular type of vegetable oil has entered the mainstream packaged food supply.

Palm oil consumption in the United States grew from just 175,000 tonnes in the year 2000, to 1.5 million tonnes by 2017–18. The European Union also saw a leap in palm oil consumption, from 2.8 million tonnes in 2000, to a massive 6.6 million by 2017–18. But it is the Asian countries – China and India in particular, consuming over 8.5 million and 10 million tonnes respectively – that are really driving the demand for palm oil. Here, highly processed foodstuffs, such as instant noodles, are forming an increasingly popular part of the daily diet, in place of fresher, more locally sourced ingredients.

The two countries most closely associated with the production of palm oil are Indonesia and Malaysia. The oil palm, the crop that produces the oil, grows best in a warm and wet tropical environment, and Indonesia and Malaysia provide the optimum conditions. The two countries exported 26 million and 16 million tonnes of palm oil respectively in 2016, significantly more than other producers, such as Guatemala (700,000 tonnes), Benin (580,000) and Papua New Guinea (560,000).

The global land area used for growing oil palm grew from 6 million to 17 million hectares (15 million to 42 million acres) between 1990 and 2012, much of it at the expense of primary tropical rainforest. Enormous forest fires are often started intentionally in order to destroy the native rainforest and clear the land in preparation for agricultural crops such as oil palm. The drastic removal of this rainforest has led to the release of significant carbon emissions, with fires in September 2015 emitting more carbon dioxide than the entire US economy in a year. It has also led to the widespread eradication of natural habitats on the Southeast Asian islands of Sumatra and Borneo for endangered species such as orangutans, rhinos, tigers and elephants.

On the plus side, oil palm produces as much as ten times more oil than alternatives such as sunflower or rapeseed oil. Given the area of land that would therefore be required for clearance in order to produce a similar volume of a competing oil, palm oil is perhaps the least damaging of all the options. This is especially the case if the palm oil is produced using more environmentally friendly initiatives, such as those used by the small, but growing, RSPO sustainable palm oil label. With the global demand for vegetable oil looking unlikely to decrease – global production of all vegetable oils grew from 90 million tonnes in 2000 to 185 million in 2017 – the large-scale adoption of more sustainable growing methods is of vital importance.

The 3 leading producers, importers and exporters of palm oil. Figures shown in thousand tonnes.

Import	Production	Export

India
10,600,000

Indonesia
38,500,000

Indonesia
28,000,000

European Union
6,500,000

Malaysia
20,500,000

Malaysia
17,250,000

China
4,900,000

Thailand
2,700,000

Guatemala
710,000

Netflix

Number of hours of available content, by country.

1000   3000

Total hours available to stream

0%   75% 100%

Percentage of available content produced domestically

Netflix

Compared to the majority of young technological upstarts with whom they find themselves rubbing shoulders, Netflix is a relative veteran of Silicon Valley. Its roots date back to August 1997, when VHS tapes were commonplace and dial-up internet and mobile phones were in their infancy. Reed Hastings and Marc Randolph, founders of Netflix, had the revolutionary idea of becoming the world's first online DVD rental store, introducing a regular subscription model in 1999. By 2007, internet speeds had developed to the point where video-on-demand became a viable business opportunity, allowing the company to move away from physical rentals. From 2013, new content creation became the next big opportunity, spawning such high-profile TV series as *Orange is the New Black* and *Stranger Things*. There are plans to spend $8 billion on new shows in 2018.

Netflix now has 125 million subscribers worldwide, enjoys a revenue of more than $11 billion and has received multiple Academy Awards, Emmy Awards and Golden Globes. As it shifts from being purely a technology company to a media company, its rivals are now increasingly mega corporations such as Disney, who are taking steps which echo Netflix's business model. In 2017, Hastings commented that Netflix's competition was not any other streaming service, but in fact their audience's willingness to just keep watching. 'When you watch a show from Netflix and you get addicted to it, you stay up late at night,' he said. 'We're competing with sleep.'

With 56.7 million domestic subscribers, the United States is comfortably the company's biggest market, although the international membership, currently at 68.3 million, is growing quickly. As the service has gradually expanded to become available in almost every country, 2017 saw international streaming outstrip domestic streaming – an indication of the rapid globalization of the company's audience. By 2022, while subscribers in the United States are expected to grow slightly to 59 million, 10 million subscribers are anticipated in the UK, 7 million in Canada, and 6 million in Brazil, plus many more around the globe. To date, other regions of the world have been slower to get on board, with only 6 million subscribers currently across the entire Asia-Pacific, and little more than 2 million across all of Africa and the Middle East.

Despite being a global company with, in theory, globally shared content, there is great disparity between the volume of content available in different countries. In the United States a total of 5,680 videos were available in January 2016, the vast majority produced domestically. This is in part due to the US being Netflix's home audience, but perhaps primarily due to the large, very wealthy television production industry in the US, which has been pivotal in shaping television broadcasting globally for decades. Hence, viewers in other major markets such as the UK, Australia and Japan mainly consume American-made programming on Netflix, and on average only occasionally watch homegrown content.

Perhaps with this in mind, in April 2018 the company launched a massive upscaling in content production from new countries and in different languages, with more than 100 new projects from sixteen countries – including Denmark, Georgia, Lebanon and South Africa – broadcasting in languages such as Arabic, Catalan, Hebrew and Turkish. After twenty years in business, Netflix's ambitions are now firmly focused on conquering the world.

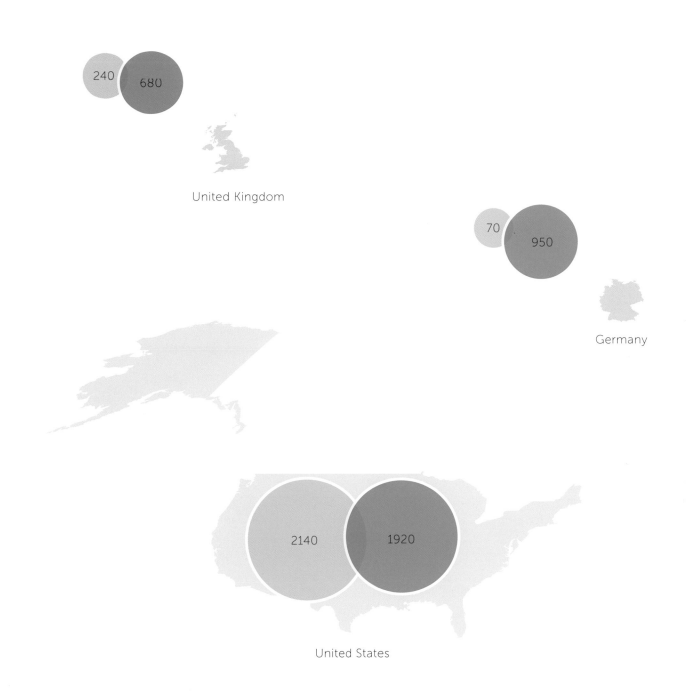

240

680

United Kingdom

70

950

Germany

2140

1920

United States

Number of hours of available Amazon Prime content, by country, and the percentage of available content produced domestically. Amazon Prime content creation in the US occurs at such a rapid pace that, unlike other countries, there is more Amazon programming created in the US than American viewers actually have access to watch.

Hours produced

Hours available

Remittances: Europe

The leading outflow nations.

- France
- Germany
- Italy
- Luxembourg
- Netherlands
- Switzerland
- United Kingdom

The inflow and outflow of the 5 largest remittance receivers

Total inflow ← → Total outflow

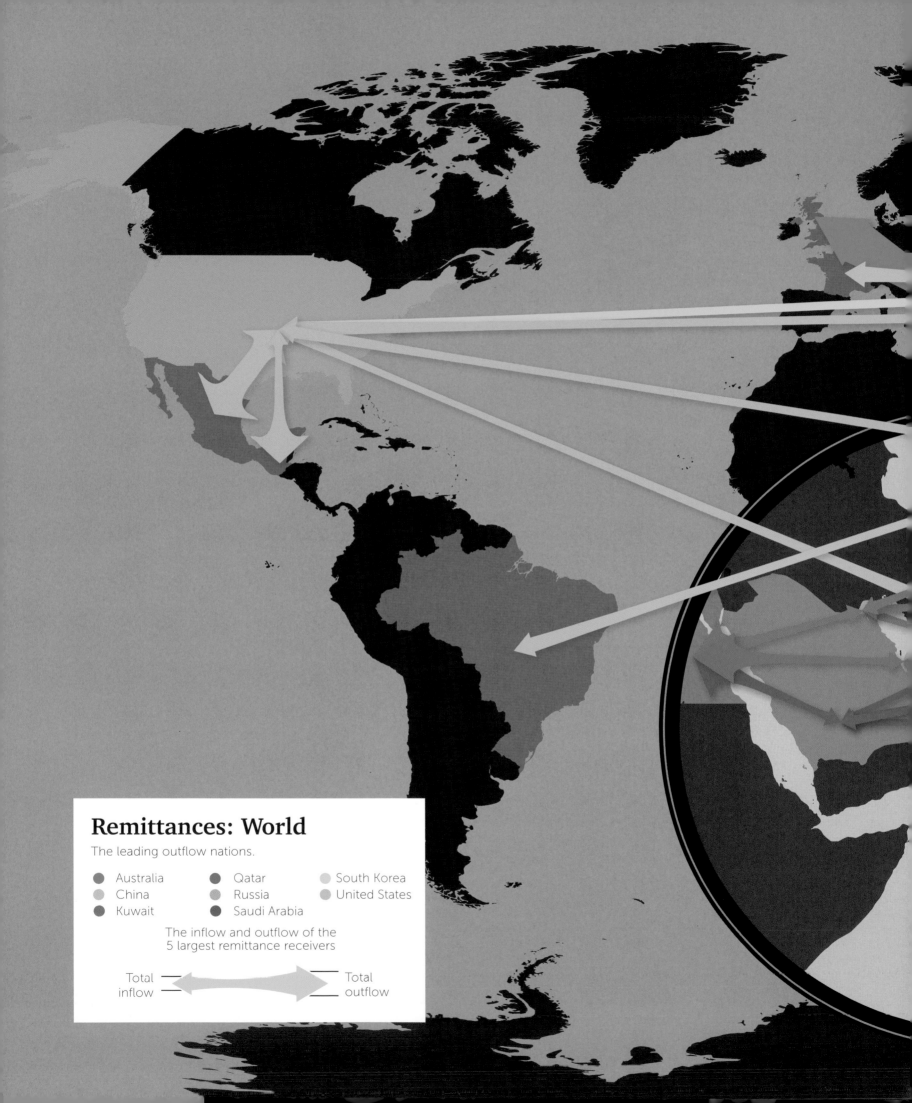

Remittances: World

The leading outflow nations.

- ● Australia
- ● China
- ● Kuwait
- ● Qatar
- ● Russia
- ● Saudi Arabia
- ● South Korea
- ● United States

The inflow and outflow of the
5 largest remittance receivers

Total inflow ◄━━━━━━━━► Total outflow

Remittances

Indirectly, money generated in more developed nations of the world sustains the lives of people in poorer nations – and this now happens on a massive scale. For many millions of people, the main source of income is not regular work, but money sent back from family members working overseas, known as remittances. The World Bank reports that remittances to developing nations totalled an incredible $466 billion in 2017, and continue to grow year after year.

For example, every year hundreds of thousands of young men leave the remote Central Asian nation of Tajikistan and endure a long journey across the border to try to find employment in Russia, where wages can be three or four times higher than back home. Despite the potential hardships, the popularity of this migration corridor means that Tajikistan is one of the world's most remittance-dependent countries, these payments supplying nearly half of its entire national income.

Tajikistan is not the only country to receive a staggering proportion of its entire national income from overseas. Countries such as the Gambia, Liberia, Comoros, Moldova, Tonga, Haiti and Nepal – all relatively poor countries, but with far larger and richer neighbours – receive more than 20 per cent of their national income from remittances. The country currently most dependent on remittance payments is now Kyrgyzstan, with $2.5 billion – more than one-third of national GDP – coming from overseas. In terms of pure numbers, the largest recipient countries of remittance payments are now India and China — receiving $62.7 billion and $61 billion respectively — followed by others with large overseas diasporas, including the Philippines, Pakistan, Mexico and Nigeria. However, many of these countries have substantially larger economies than, for example, Tajikistan, and are therefore not as dependent on remittances.

Migrants around the world can end up in backbreaking work, such as construction, agriculture or maintenance, often facing harsh working conditions, racism, police brutality and employers happy to withhold passports and even salaries. They do all this in the hope of earning enough to both sustain themselves and be able to send money back to their wives and children. For people utterly reliant on these flows of money, any unforeseen disruptions, such as economic downturns in foreign countries or extra-strict immigration laws in developed countries, can have a seriously detrimental impact on their financial security and quality of life. For example, declines in the Russian economy in recent years saw a significant drop in the size of

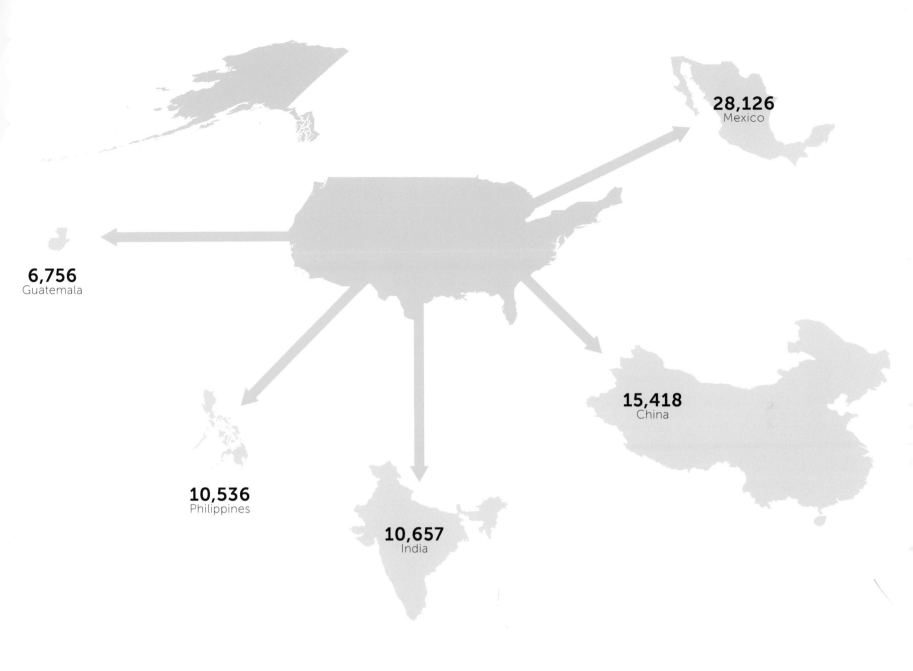

28,126
Mexico

6,756
Guatemala

15,418
China

10,536
Philippines

10,657
India

Neighbours Mexico might receive the largest amount of money sent out of the United States – the leading country for remittance outflow – but significant amounts of money also find their way to China, India, the Philippines and Guatemala. Figures shown in million US$.

remittances arriving into neighbouring countries such as Azerbaijan, Uzbekistan and Turkmenistan. Tajikistan's huge remittance dependency saw an especially painful drop, with hundreds of millions of anticipated dollars simply never arriving, a crisis for the thousands of family members dependent on these hard-earned yet unregulated payments.

Despite such fragilities, optimistic economic growth forecasts around the world, combined with anticipated increasing global migration, means remittances will continue to be a large and likely growing factor in the development prospects of millions. Whether this will prove to be the lifeline that helps reduce poverty and bring relative economic equality to a highly unequal world, or an unstable bubble poised to burst at any moment, will only be assessed by the test of time.

Diamonds

The world's diamond producers.

10 ‚ 150m
Volume, carats

Diamonds

The word 'diamonds' may conjure up thoughts of romance, expensive jewellery, perhaps an engagement. It's unlikely, however, to prompt visions of an obscure port city in India, where the state of Gujarat meets the Arabian Sea. This city – Surat – sits at the very centre of the world's polished-diamond industry, despite the fact that India does not actually produce any diamonds itself. However, in Surat, half a million or more people are currently employed in businesses that are directly tied to the global diamond supply.

Unlike India, Russia has enormous diamond reserves – currently at least a whopping 650 million carats, easily the biggest reserves in the world. One carat is equal to 0.2 grams, although weight is not the only factor, since larger diamonds are often more valuable than many smaller diamonds of the same weight. The Democratic Republic of the Congo (DRC), with 150 million carats, and Australia, with 120 million carats, have the next biggest reserves. Like all diamonds, the minerals will have formed some 250km (155 miles) underground over many hundreds of millions of years, the result of a combination of intense heat and pressure. In 2016, Russia mined 18 million carats of rough diamonds, primarily in remote Siberia. The only single country to top this volume was the DRC, which mined 19 million carats. Together, the two countries contributed almost one-third of the total global production of diamonds that year, which stood at 127 million carats.

In order to turn this mineral into a shiny and extremely expensive commodity, rough diamonds are 'cut' through a process that involves grinding and polishing. And there is no better place in the world to cut diamonds than Surat. The city's monopoly has swollen during the course of the twentieth century; by 2016 as much as 90 per cent of the world's diamond cutting took place there. Once cut, newly polished diamonds embark on international travels to renowned diamond retail hubs such as New York, Antwerp and Dubai.

The popularity of the diamond business in this region – besides the obvious sizeable profits on offer – owes much to the unique culture of the

90%

Surat, India, sits at the very centre of the world's diamond trade.

region, specifically that of the Jain community. For these strict vegans, the traditional trades associated with agriculture that are found across much of the rest of India are out of bounds career-wise. The more the Jains chose to pursue diamond cutting as a business, the more Surat overtook potential competitors from other countries.

In 2013, global sales of polished diamonds topped a healthy $22 billion. Despite the rosy picture this may paint, the future of the diamond industry is not short of concern. With an increasingly rich array of sports cars, designer bags, clothes and shoes, and technological devices entering the marketplace, diamond jewellery is not the only luxury product competing for the chequebooks of the very wealthy, and there is evidence that demands for such expensive jewellery is waning. Instead, diamond producers may need to consider manufacturing as an alternative destination for their wares – as one of the hardest natural materials, diamond fragments are very important for use as abrasives and drill bits – although the prospect of lab-grown diamonds entering the supply chain means even this is no safe bet. The future of the diamond industry is far from crystal clear.

Sneakers

Leading countries by revenue of the athletic footwear market, and top exporters to the highest revenue market, the US.

| 10m | 100m | 200m | 500m | 1b | 2.5b | 5b | 15b |

US$

Less   More

Ireland
1.34

United States
0.95

Sneakers

Offering welcome protection for our feet as we traverse from A to B, and increasingly seen as a fashion statement on which to lavish great sums of money, shoes also provide one of the key indicators of the global economy. Sneakers, or trainers in the United Kingdom, in particular, have become a symbol of the new, globalized world that has evolved over recent decades.

One country that has emerged as a major player in the manufacture of athletic shoes is Vietnam. The country started exporting shoes in 1992 – mainly to Eastern Europe – and in 1995, American sports-footwear giant Nike contracted five Vietnamese footwear factories to produce their distinctively branded sneakers, clear evidence that the country was firmly on the shoemaking map. By 2016, more than 1.2 billion pairs of sneakers were being produced in Vietnam, with more than one billion shipped abroad at a value of over $15 billion. As these figures indicate, the financial return per shoe is relatively low, since the competitive advantage the country has over potential rivals is a low minimum wage and therefore a cheap labour force. Unfortunately, this makes it hard for workers to grow skills beyond the basic labour required for stitching shoes together. This is especially a problem with the uncertainty of robotic automation constantly looming in the background, threatening to rob the estimated one million Vietnamese working in shoe assembly – around 80 per cent of whom are women – of their delicate livelihoods.

Overall, the athletic shoe industry sold 900 million pairs of shoes in 2017, worth a staggering $47 billion. Comprising roughly 15 per cent of the global

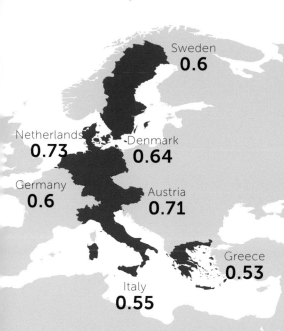

Sweden
0.6

Netherlands
0.73

Denmark
0.64

Germany
0.6

Austria
0.71

Greece
0.53

Italy
0.55

Singapore
0.55

Irish shoppers are the world's biggest purchasers, with the average person buying more pairs of athletic footwear than the United States, Austria or the Netherlands. Figures show per-capita volume sales in the athletic footwear market, in number of pairs.

footwear industry, this is an incredible leap from the $16 billion it was worth back in 2010. Nike and Adidas are the two biggest players in this business, with Nike generating global sales of over $23 billion in 2017, and Adidas selling more than $15 billion's worth. These two giants also own numerous other major brands, such as Converse for Nike and Reebok for Adidas, making each other their only significant competitors. With the sporting heritages of these brands increasingly hybridizing with the eclectic and profitable world of fashion, there should perhaps be no surprise that the athletic shoe market is anticipated to reach $68 billion by 2021.

This projected worth highlights the economic imbalances behind such industries. The Vietnamese, despite manufacturing such a high proportion of sneakers, spend essentially nothing on buying sneakers themselves. Perhaps surprisingly, globally, Ireland is home to the biggest athletic shoe fanatics, being the only country where the average citizen bought more than one pair of sneakers in 2017, spending around $45 each. Other countries happy to splash the cash when it comes to sporting footwear were Austria, the United States, the Netherlands and Denmark.

The incredible number of shoes being produced, bought and sold around the world every year is a reminder of the complicated network behind manufacturing the humble sneaker, which makes the athletic shoe industry among the most globalized of all household items.

SNEAKERS

69

Cement

Leading countries in worldwide cement production.

100　　　　　　　　　　　　　　2400

Tonnes

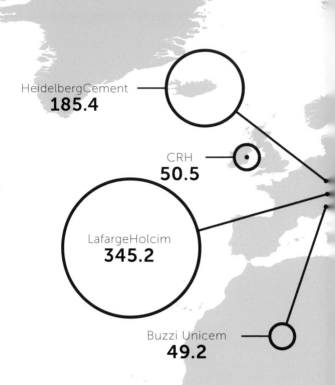

HeidelbergCement
185.4

CRH
50.5

LafargeHolcim
345.2

Buzzi Unicem
49.2

Cemex
91.6

Dangote Cement
43.8

Cement

Try as we might, it's impossible to conceive of the modern world without concrete. Skyscrapers surge towards the sky, lengthy bridges span vast rivers and valleys and coasts around the world are capable of withstanding the relentless ebb and flow of waves, all thanks to the stability that concrete provides. Ultimately, the urban landscape is entirely reliant upon it.

A patent for cement, the key component of concrete, was awarded to Joseph Asplin, of Leeds, UK, in 1824. Registering his new synthetic construction material, comprised of limestone and clay, he named it 'portland cement' (in reference to the popular limestone construction material 'portland stone' from Dorset, in the south of England). Whether Asplin is the true inventor of cement – there are certainly other contenders for the title – the opportunities presented by this new material saw it become a mainstay of the Industrial Revolution. Its use spread quickly across Europe and North America and then, in the twentieth century, around the rest of the world.

In 2014 alone, nearly 4.2 billion tonnes of cement were produced globally, over half of it in China (around 250 million tonnes produced in India, with the rest spread out around the world). Despite being the world's biggest producer of cement, China exports only a small proportion of it, less than 18 million tons (which still makes them the world's largest exporter, far ahead of Japan and Turkey, the next highest). The vast majority of China's cement is used domestically, for the many urbanisation and infrastructure projects currently underway across the country.

It is only when mixed with sand, gravel and water, that cement can be turned into concrete for use in construction. When considering the huge figures relating to the trade in cement, therefore, it is possible to estimate the quantities of these other aggregates – the sand and the gravel necessary to

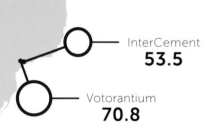

InterCement
53.5

Votorantium
70.8

Eurocement
47.2

UltraTech Cement
91.4

Swiss company
LafargeHolcim are the
world's largest producers
of cement.

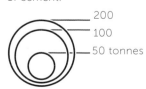

200
100
50 tonnes

satisfy the current global demands for concrete production. Both materials are used in quantities six to seven times that of cement, and the UN Environment Programme estimates between 25.9 billion and 29.6 billion tonnes of aggregate were mined for concrete in 2012 alone – resulting in enough concrete to build a wall 27m high by 27m wide (89 x 89ft) around the equator. Unfortunately, the sand found in huge volumes in the world's deserts is too smooth for construction purposes. Instead, it has to be sourced from beaches. In recent years, this has put immense pressure on countries from Cambodia to India and from Australia to Kenya, as entire coastlines are dredged and exported, to be turned into concrete.

Modern concrete is known to deteriorate over time, particularly that used for coastal defences, which constantly have to withstand bombardment by the ocean. Conversely, 2,000-year-old Roman concrete has truly withstood the test of time, and can still be seen along coasts around the Mediterranean. Unfortunately, the formula for such long-lasting concrete was lost when Rome collapsed. But, in 2017, a team of researchers from the University of Utah in the United States developed what they believe might be the secret recipe, a combination of volcanic ash, lime and seawater. After two hundred years of revolution in the construction industry, concrete might just be set as the favoured building material for one more.

Global Debt

Public debt as a percentage of gross domestic product (GDP), by country.

1   50   100   250

% of GDP

240%

100%

5%

10 countries
with highest and
lowest debt, as
percentage of GDP

Global Debt

The invisible network of debt that stretches around the world has become so vast and complicated that it's a challenge for economists, not to mention regulators, to keep track of. Almost every country in the world carries with it a significant national debt – a constant outgoing of funds to pay for everything from transport and infrastructure to pensions, emergency services and the military. What complicates the situation is that many countries lend money to each other and therefore owe money to each other. For example, Japan, one of the most indebted countries, is also one of the biggest creditors, alongside China, to the United States.

As the world has slowly and gradually recovered from the debilitating effects of the 2008 global economic crash (where public debts soared as governments borrowed vast sums in order to prevent their biggest financial institutions from crashing the entire economy) global debt has continued to climb. In 2006, prior to the crash, global debt was relatively stable, hovering at around $26 trillion in total. Yet post-crash, even as the world's economy returned to growth, the world's governments had borrowed so much money to bail out their financial institutions that the scale of debt just kept rising. By 2017, a decade after the crash, the figure had more than doubled – to an eye-watering $60 trillion – and it continues to climb.

Japan leads the list of countries driving up this debt bubble, with an immense public debt exceeding 239.3 per cent of the size of the country's economy (as measured by GDP). Famously suffering from the early stages of an ageing population, which places great demands upon public finances to support a growing number of retirees, Japan has spent much of the past two decades stuck in this situation, with government after government trying to balance the budget. The countries currently experiencing the next highest levels of debt are Greece (181.6 per cent), Lebanon (148.7 per cent) and Italy (132.6 per cent) – all countries with ageing populations.

Though it sounds extreme, these countries are not alone. Plenty of the world's richest nations have public debts equal to, or in excess of, their total GDP, largely as a direct result of the 2008 crash. In the United States, public debt, a mere $5.7 trillion at the turn of the millennium, had grown to a massive $20.2 trillion by 2017. The country's need to raise the national debt ceiling to avoid nationwide government shutdowns is now a semi-regular event in the national calendar.

There is an extremely diverse collection of nations at the other end of the table, with Afghanistan, Estonia, the Solomon Islands and Botswana among those with the lowest national debts. The ability to balance the books means that, while none of these countries happen to have particularly large economies, they can at least be considered stable, with sensible investments being made with public funds that deliver healthy returns. But it is Brunei, the microstate of 440,000 people located on the island of Borneo, that has the world's lowest debt, just 3 per cent. The reason for this is simple: oil, which makes up two-thirds of its national GDP. With the high revenues generated by the hydrocarbons industry, Bruneian banks are capable of funding this relatively small economy, instead of relying on loans from other countries to stay in the red, as many other nations do.

Portugal

Cape Verde

Senegal

The geographic spread of the 10 countries with the highest and lowest public debt.

Estonia

Russia

Kazakhstan

Italy

Uzbekistan

Greece

Lebanon

Afghanistan

Saudi Arabia

Bhutan

Japan

Republic
of Congo

Eritrea

Brunei

Democratic
Republic of
Congo

Botswana

Soloman
Islands

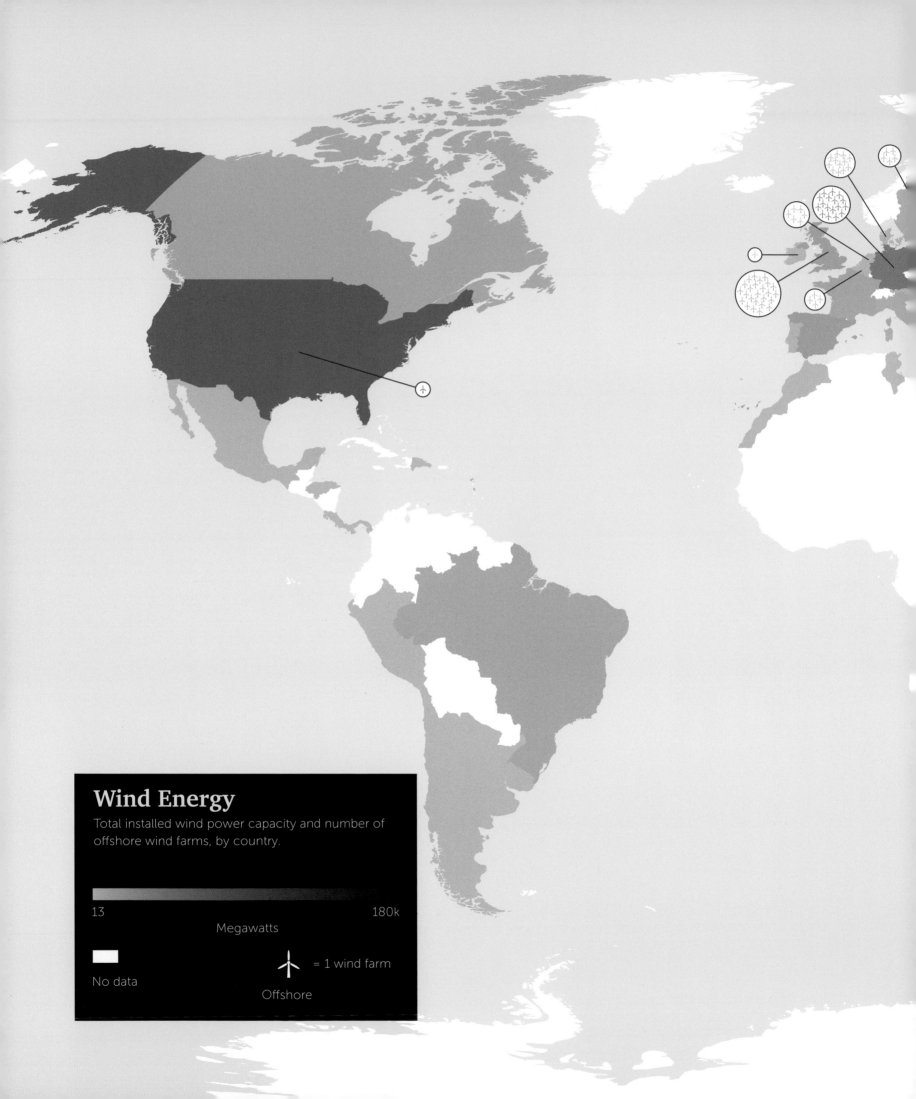

Wind Energy

Total installed wind power capacity and number of offshore wind farms, by country.

13   180k

Megawatts

No data

= 1 wind farm

Offshore

Wind Energy

In 1885, Scottish academic James Blyth decided to test his controversial theory that, instead of relying on non-renewable fuels such as wood, coal and oil, humans could harness the natural energy of the wind to power their increasingly energy-demanding lives. He constructed a 10m (33ft) turbine with large canvas sails, and erected it in the garden of his cottage in Marykirk, Aberdeenshire. Eventually, he perfected a system that was able to deliver wind-generated electricity to his house, a set-up that operated successfully for over twenty-five years.

It may have been a fluke of birth that Blyth found himself operating in this remote corner of Britain, but he could hardly have chosen a better place in the whole world. Located on the fringes of the large Eurasian landmass, with the Atlantic Ocean to the east, the Arctic Ocean to the north, and subjected to constantly changing atmospheric pressures, the British Isles are among the windiest parts of the inhabited world. Strong winds blow in from almost any direction, although southwesterly winds prevail. These factors combine with the impact of the fast-moving jet stream, which moves weather systems around the globe, to make the United Kingdom a front-runner in the race to become the world's wind-energy powerhouse.

In 2017, the United Kingdom's offshore wind-power capacity reached 6.8 gigawatts (Gw), out of a global capacity of 18.8 Gw. Henrik Poulsen, CEO of DONG Energy (now Ørsted), the UK's largest wind-farm operator, is on record stating that he believes wind energy could soon power the entire country. Thanks to an optimal geographical location and long-term infrastructural investments, the United Kingdom is currently the world leader in offshore wind-energy generation, with twenty-five offshore wind farms as of October 2017, and a further four under construction. By comparison, Germany has seventeen (with four under construction) and China has thirteen (with seven under construction).

When it comes to onshore wind energy, it is China that takes the lead globally, generating 161 Gw annually. By comparison, the United States generates 87.5 Gw and the United Kingdom 12.9 Gw. Overall, the world constructed sufficient infrastructure to be able to generate 540 Gw of wind energy in 2017, around 4 per cent of global electricity demand. It's a rapid increase from just 24.3 Gw in 2001, reflecting the plummeting costs involved in generation, and therefore the dedication of successive governments and energy companies to wind as a viable energy source.

Crucially, this power doesn't always stay entirely within the country in which it is generated. Thanks to an existing network of interconnectors and the potential – in the future, at least – to use offshore islands to store energy, neighbouring countries are able to benefit from the renewable, low-carbon energy as well. In the case of the United Kingdom, this could mean wind power generated within the British Isles eventually being consumed by neighbours including France, the Netherlands, Ireland, Belgium or Norway. It may have taken over a century, but Blyth's dream of a wind-powered world might finally be on the horizon.

Distribution of the United
Kingdom's offshore wind
farms.

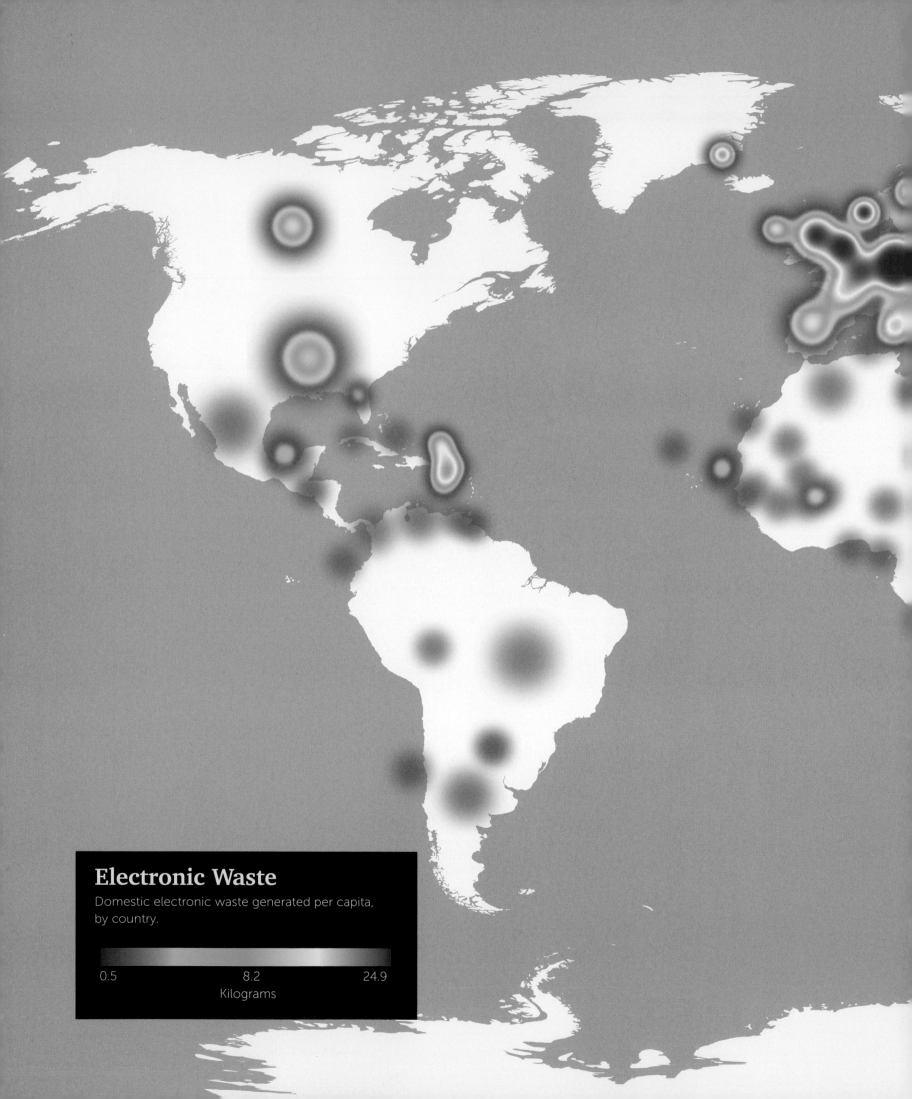

Electronic Waste

Domestic electronic waste generated per capita, by country.

0.5	8.2	24.9

Kilograms

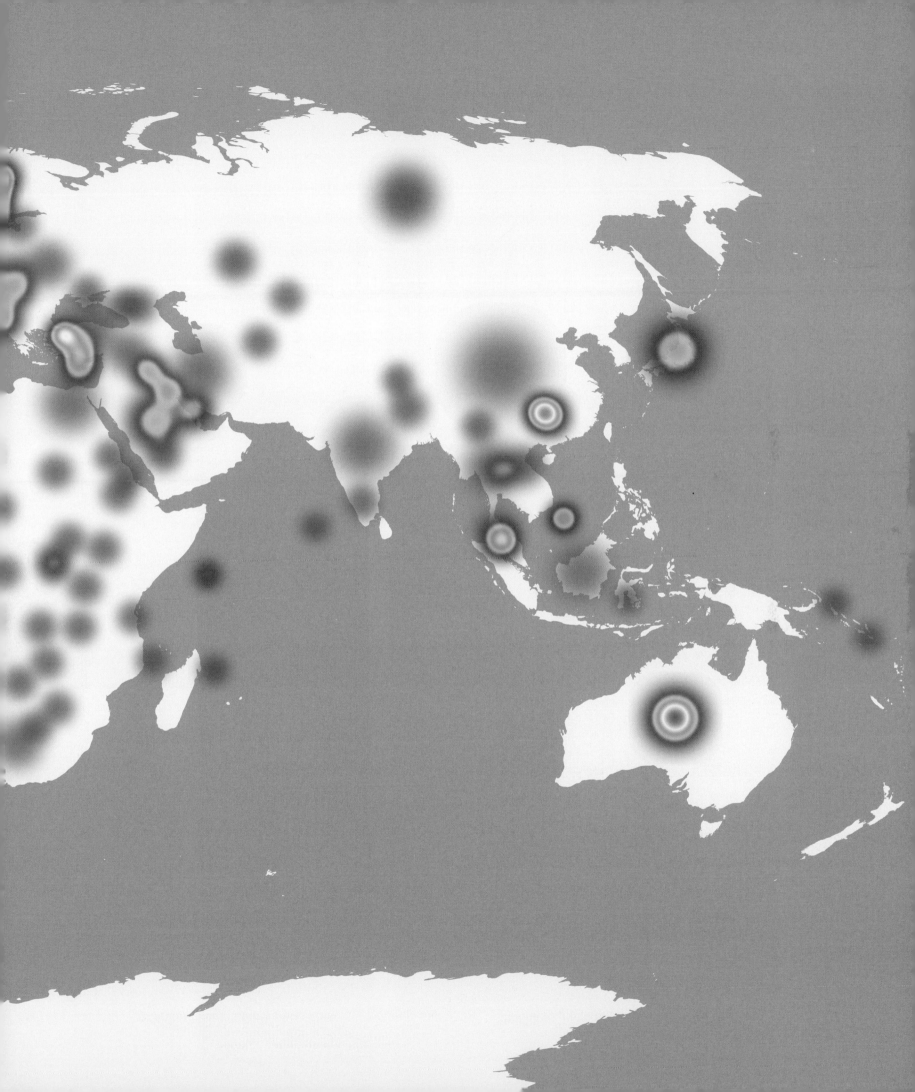

Electronic Waste

Look around any modern twenty-first century home, and it's likely to be scattered with mobile phones, computers, televisions, cooking appliances, and any number of other electronic devices. Produced for a fraction of what they would have cost even a few years earlier, getting our hands on new versions or the next best thing has never been so easy.

There are few places in the world where the growth in such devices hasn't changed or even radically revolutionized daily life. Unfortunately, this rapid technological shift, combined with the speed at which devices break or become obsolete, has also led to an exponential global increase in electronic waste, known as 'e-waste'. Between 2010 and 2018, the overall amount of e-waste generated by the world climbed from 33.8 million tonnes to 49.8 million. Europe is the driving force behind this rise, in terms of the individual contribution of each person, with Norway (28.5kg/62¾lb per person), the UK (24.9kg/55lb), Denmark (24.8kg/54¾lb) and the Netherlands (23.9kg/52¾lb) leading the way.

However, the population size of Asian countries (and the growing numbers of wealthy consumers there) mean that nations in this part of the world are exceeding the e-waste of European countries. Japan and India, for example, generate 2.1 million and 2 million tonnes respectively each year. Yet these countries are dwarfed by their neighbour, China, which creates over 7.2 million tonnes of e-waste every single year.

One obvious answer to e-waste is to promote recycling of devices, especially since materials such as gold, silver, palladium, copper and other valuable metals, often found in small quantities within cables and/or circuit boards, remain highly desirable resources, yet are nevertheless thrown away in large quantities. Recycling rates for e-waste remain stubbornly stagnant in many developed economies; even countries such as Denmark and Norway, with rates of around 42 per cent and 47 per cent respectively, have seen little change over the past decade.

Several countries, many in Southeast Asia, such as Cambodia, Indonesia and Thailand, have no established legal framework for e-waste management, and instead have witnessed the growth of informal practices of e-waste dumping and 'backyard recycling' – the crude use of acid baths and open burning to extract traces of the valuable metals left inside. As well as polluting the environment by releasing hazardous chemicals, these practices also often produce toxic fumes, resulting in severe health problems.

On the other hand, countries such as Japan, South Korea and Taiwan are succeeding in raising their game at eliminating the technological waste they generate, with all three having established sophisticated e-waste collection and recycling systems as far back as the 1990s. Through a combination of strong government oversight and opportunistic entrepreneurship, innovative ideas such as special recycling funds, household appliance return schemes and enforced pay-per-bag disposal have turned former refuse sites into clean parks and recreation areas. By viewing e-waste as a resource, not a burden, these densely populated countries have paved a way forwards for the rest of the world.

Despite the boom in new electronic gadgets, it is standard household appliances which currently produce the most e-waste globally. Figures show volume of waste in million tonnes.

 Small equipment: vaccum cleaners, microwaves, toasters, video cameras. electronic toys

 Large equipment: washing machines, electric stoves, large printing machines

 Temperature exchange equipment: refrigerators, freezers, air conditioners

 Screens: televisions, monitors, laptops, tablets

 Small IT: mobile phones, printers, GPS devices

 Lamps: fluorescent, high intensity discharge, LED

16.8　**9.2**　**7.6**　**6.6**　**3.9**　**0.7**

Ports

The leading 100 global ports, by annual throughput.

1.5m   35m

Twenty-foot equivalent units (teus)

35
10
1.5 million

Sized by teu

Ports

Operating on a scale we can scarcely comprehend, the world's ports play a central role in the global movement of goods, facilitating the transportation of thousands of ships out at sea at any one time, carrying everything from clothes, oil and televisions to cars, home appliances and boxes of food around the world. Hundreds of International Maritime Organization (IMO) designated marine highways (officially known as 'traffic separation schemes') carry as much as 97 per cent of all retailed goods from port to port. Furthermore, the volume carried is increasing. In 2016, the world's largest one hundred container ports handled 555.6 million twenty-foot containers (measured using the term 'teu', for twenty-foot equivalent unit) between them – an increase of 12 million teu on the previous year.

The figures are staggering. From a geographic angle, it's impossible to think about this shipping juggernaut without focusing on Asia, specifically China, which is home to seven of the world's ten busiest ports: Shanghai, Shenzhen, Ningbo-Zhoushan, Hong Kong, Guangzhou, Qingdao and Tianjin (the non-Chinese ports are Busan in South Korea, Dubai in the United Arab Emirates and Singapore). With more than 37 million teu, Shanghai has ranked as the world's busiest port for nearly a decade, and continues to open new facilities in order to handle bigger ships carrying ever-larger volumes of cargo. As the main maritime gate in and out of China, Shanghai handles numerous raw materials for industry, including iron ore, coal, oil, steel and various other construction materials.

Singapore's 30.9 million teu places the port as the world's second busiest, partially a result of the island's uniquely strategic geographical location in the narrow Malacca Strait sandwiched between the Malay peninsula and the Indonesian island of Sumatra. Singapore takes full advantage of this situation with its profitable transhipment model, acting as a regional hub where freight can be unloaded and reloaded before being shipped on to its final destination.

At the opposite end of the transaction from Shanghai and Shenzhen are such ports as Hamburg and Los Angeles, which provide vast entry points for shipments into their respective continents. The most significant of these remains the Dutch city of Rotterdam, with its sprawling industrial landscape. Strategically positioned between the Rhine river delta and the North Sea, Rotterdam transports 12.4 million teu of, primarily, crude oil, petroleum, grain and other commodities between Europe and the rest of the world, making it the world's twelfth largest port.

It is not every day that we consider the vital role played by the world's strategic shipping ports, since they are very rarely in the news, despite both their logistical importance and the significant impact their emissions make towards climate change (more than the entire United Kingdom). But even this far into the twenty-first century, the global economy simply couldn't function without them.

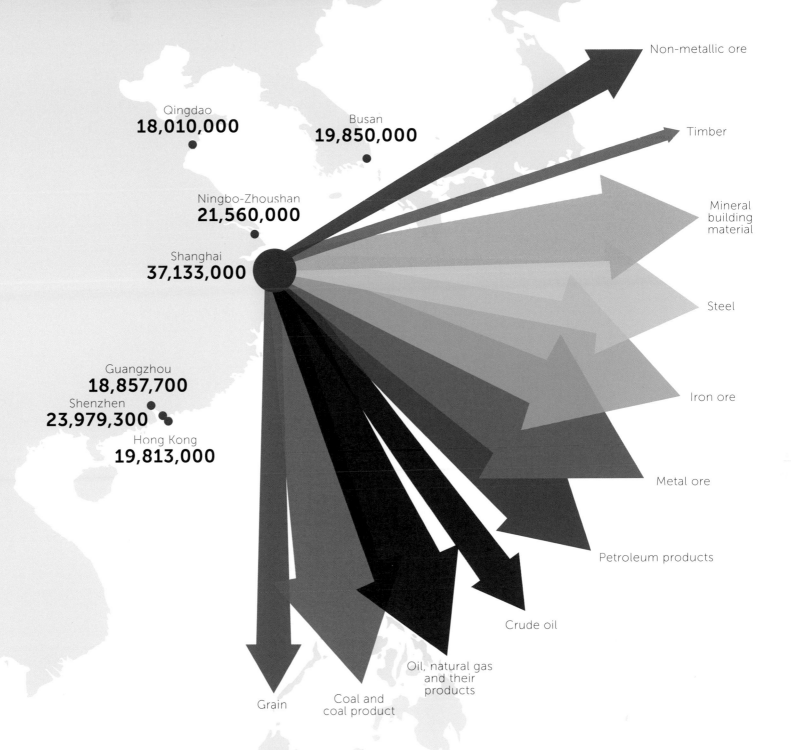

Qingdao
18,010,000

Busan
19,850,000

Non-metallic ore

Timber

Ningbo-Zhoushan
21,560,000

Mineral
building
material

Shanghai
37,133,000

Steel

Iron ore

Guangzhou
18,857,700

Shenzhen
23,979,300

Hong Kong
19,813,000

Metal ore

Petroleum products

Crude oil

Oil, natural gas
and their
products

Grain

Coal and
coal product

Singapore
30,903,600

The annual throughput,
measured in teus, of the
8 largest global ports.
Shanghai remains the top
global port for shipping
traffic, with over 37 million
teus annually, exporting
the world's essential
commodities.

Humanitarian Assistance

The largest donors and recipients of humanitarian aid worldwide.

250m	450b

Donated, US$

250m	450b

Received, US$

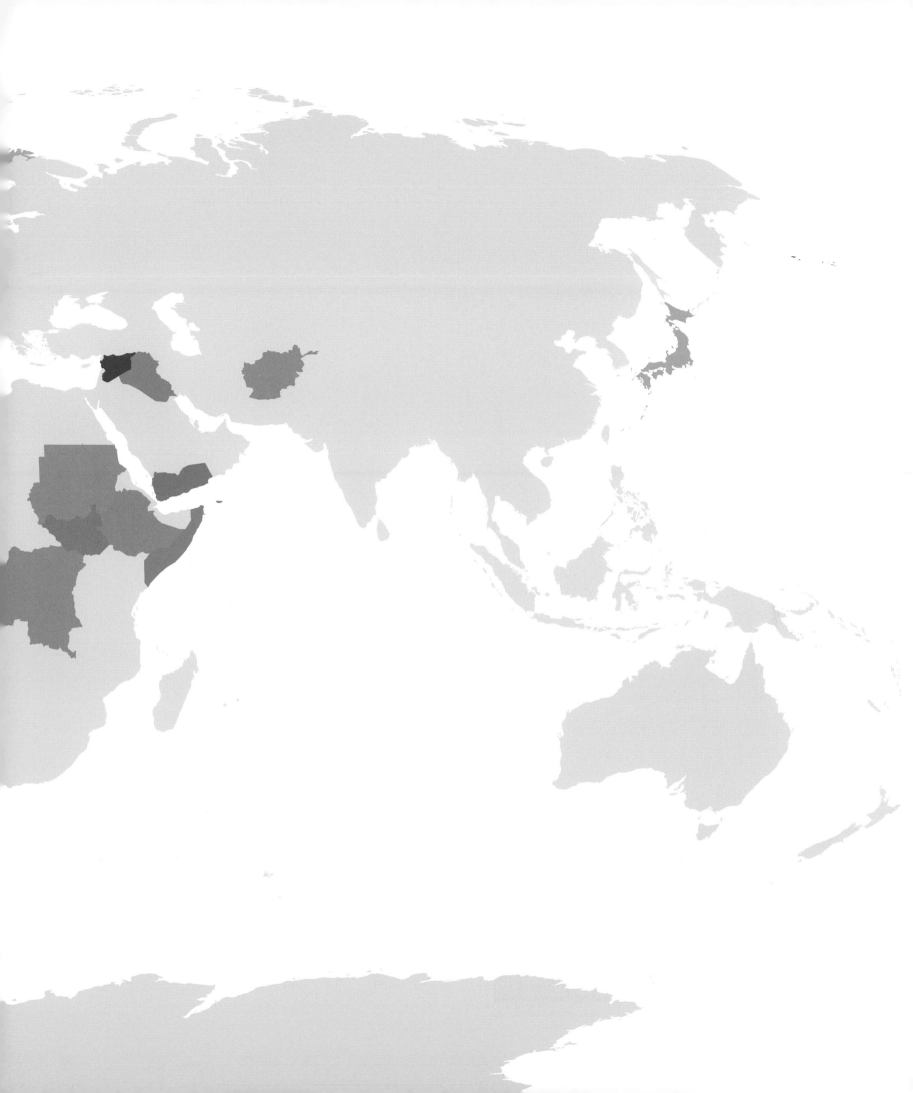

Humanitarian Assistance

In the past half decade, a rapid escalation in the amount of money made available by the world's governments for humanitarian aid has seen a dramatic rise from $11.8 billion in 2012 to $19.2 billion in 2015. While this figure continues to grow, the pace of growth appears to be levelling off. Increasingly, private donors such as wealthy philanthropists, large companies keen to demonstrate corporate social responsibility and non-government organizations that include the World Food Programme, the International Red Cross, Médecins Sans Frontières and the UN Refugee Agency are taking over from national governments in contributing vast sums towards various humanitarian development programmes.

Foreign aid can always be relied on to stimulate impassioned debate in the media about the responsibilities (or otherwise) of richer countries towards the rest of the world. Certainly, one striking observation is how few countries are involved in both the giving and receiving of the majority of funding. The vast majority of funds are donated by only a handful of national governments. The number-one donor worldwide is the United States, which gave more than $4.5 billion in 2017 – around one-third of all donations made that year. Germany donated $1.7 billion, followed by the European Commission ($1.4 billion), the United Kingdom ($1.1 billion) and Japan ($400 million), after which there is a significant drop off in donations. Sweden and Norway can perhaps be considered the most generous on an individual level, since their donations of $279 million and $247 million respectively were among the highest per person donations of the entire world.

The destination of this funding is just as concentrated, currently focusing principally on one country, Syria, with sizeable donations also going to Yemen, South Sudan, Iraq and Somalia, which have also been afflicted by crises such as ongoing conflict and drought. Syria specifically has required immense amounts of money to fund both on-the-ground humanitarian work, and the resettlement of the millions of refugees forced to flee the country, primarily to neighbouring Turkey.

As these examples tragically show, human conflict and the need for humanitarian aid are very often directly correlated, as the people most in need of aid (over 164 million people across 47 countries in 2016 being the 'best guess' from the scraps of data available) so often hail from a handful of countries where fighting remains a daily occurrence. Internal displacement also remains a less visible but severe problem that usually requires long-term external assistance. In Colombia, the legacy of half a century of civil war

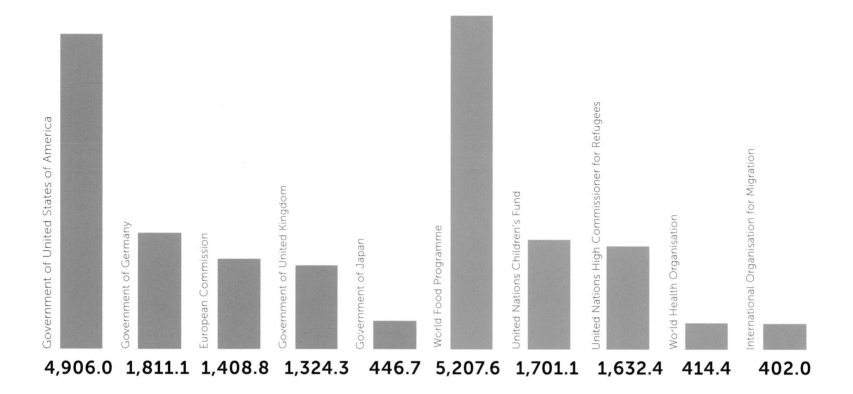

| 4,906.0 | 1,811.1 | 1,408.8 | 1,324.3 | 446.7 | 5,207.6 | 1,701.1 | 1,632.4 | 414.4 | 402.0 |

Government of United States of America · Government of Germany · European Commission · Government of United Kingdom · Government of Japan · World Food Programme · United Nations Children's Fund · United Nations High Commissioner for Refugees · World Health Organisation · International Organisation for Migration

Some of the largest non-government organisations provide as much humanitarian assistance, or more, than the wealthiest national governments. Figures are given in million US$.

means 7.2 million people remain displaced in 2016, which exceeded even the numbers leaving Syria.

In these countries, aid provided in the aftermath of extreme events, once the story has fallen out of the media, helps to maintain peace and stability, and prevent a backwards slide towards far more volatile situations. The underreported yet vital role this humanitarian aid plays helps make incremental steps towards a world in which such assistance isn't required at all.

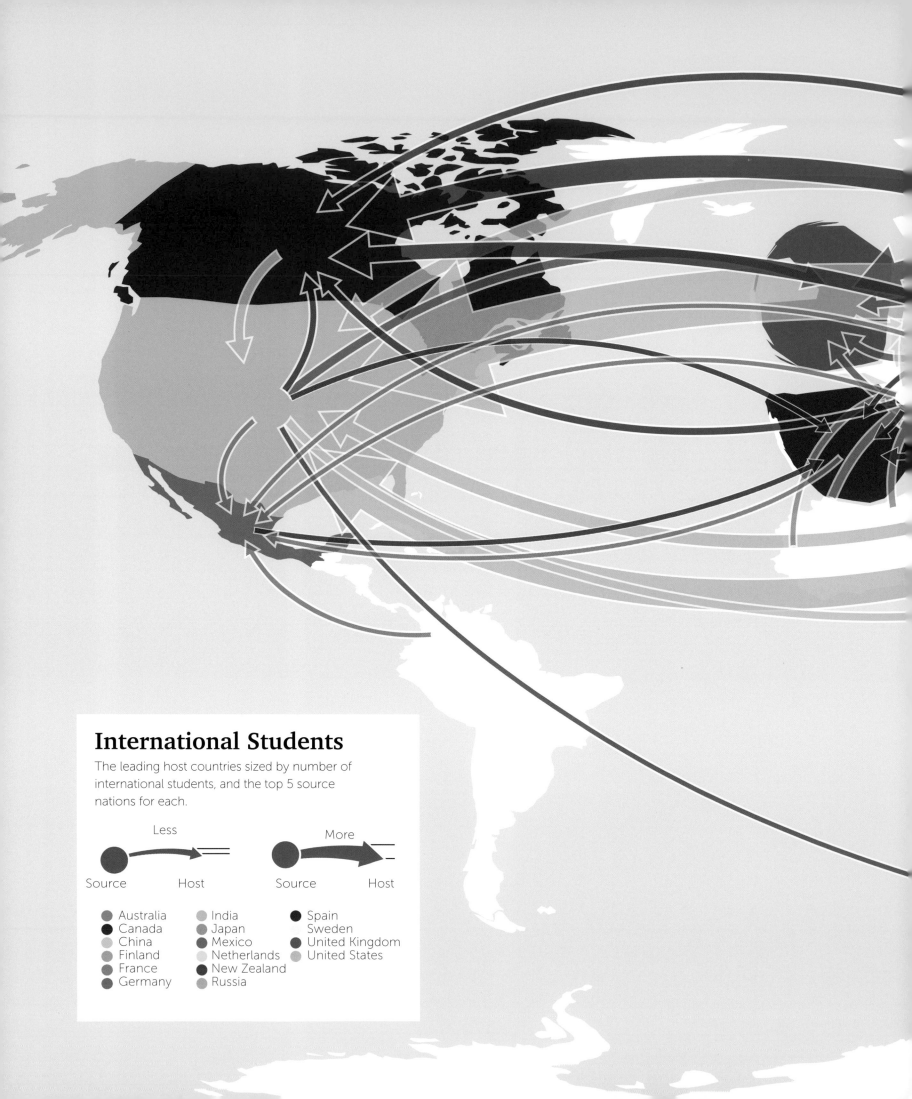

International Students

The leading host countries sized by number of international students, and the top 5 source nations for each.

Less

Source   Host

More

Source   Host

- Australia
- Canada
- China
- Finland
- France
- Germany
- India
- Japan
- Mexico
- Netherlands
- New Zealand
- Russia
- Spain
- Sweden
- United Kingdom
- United States

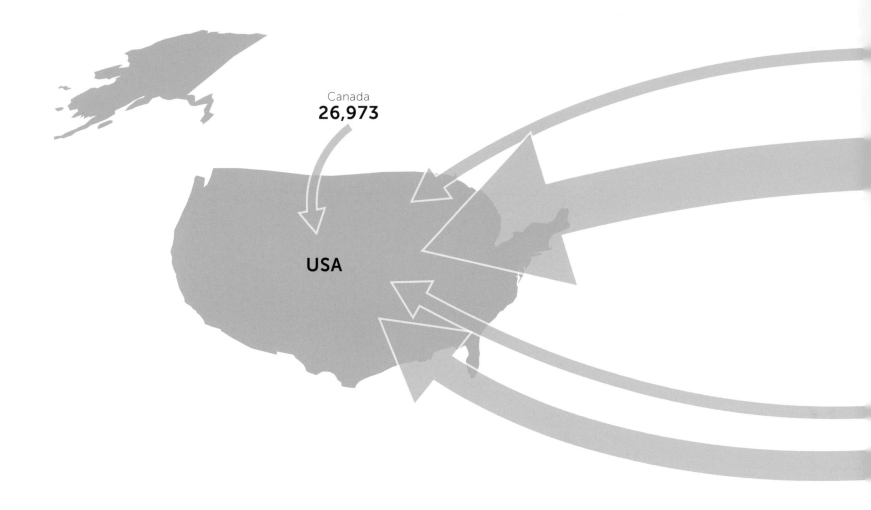

Canada
26,973

USA

International Students

The next generation is looking beyond its own borders for education like never before in history. Students take themselves thousands of miles from family and friends to grapple with the rigours of higher education, often in an unfamiliar culture, and quite probably with a language barrier thrown in for good measure. However the opportunities offered by an education at a top college – and the favourable employment and networking that may follow – are enticing millions of ambitious young people around the world to leave home and head overseas.

Few statistics tell the story more forcibly than the following: around the turn of the millennium, there were 2.1 million international students globally. Since that time, this number has more than doubled, to more than 4.6 million students, and is growing.

Predictably, the rapid development in the economies of East Asia in recent decades means countries such as South Korea and China have become the most significant players in this paradigm shift. Young Chinese now make up the single-largest student nationality (aside from domestic students) in Germany, France, New Zealand, Japan and many others, while the United Kingdom, Canada and Australia each play host to around 100,000 Chinese higher-education students annually. There is no other country whose young people have so radically revolutionized the system of higher education.

As host to the largest population of international students in the entire world, with well over 1,000,000 international students annually, the United States is also educating the largest number of Chinese students, with more than 320,000

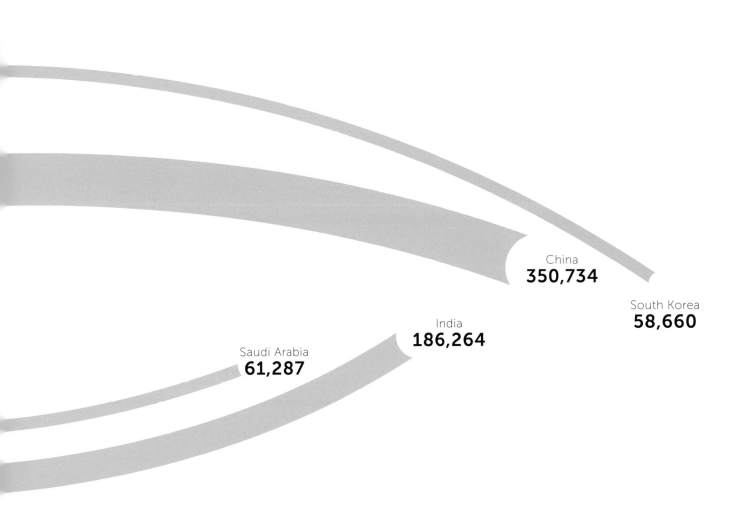

China
350,734

South Korea
58,660

India
186,264

Saudi Arabia
61,287

The 5 leading countries of origin for international students in the United States, the largest host country. Over half a million international students arrive every year, overwhelmingly from China and India.

choosing to travel to the United States every year to study (up from 65,000 or so only a decade ago). While Chinese students are therefore comfortably the highest overseas nationality currently studying in the country – above such nations as India, Canada and Saudi Arabia – the sheer numbers of higher-education students in the States mean that even this vast international cohort makes up only around 5 per cent of the total number of students in the country. At the other end of the spectrum, Australia stands out as educating the largest ratio of international-versus-domestic students, with more than one-quarter of all their higher-education students coming from overseas. Typically these are students from regional neighbours such as India, Malaysia, Vietnam, Nepal and China.

Significantly, China is itself increasingly becoming a popular host for international students

– evidence of the country's rising importance on the world stage, and the respectability of Chinese academic institutions such as Beijing's Peking University and Tsinghua University, both inside the top thirty of the 2018 World University Rankings. While the sizeable domestic population means that only one per cent of China's higher-education students are from outside the country, it hosts around ten per cent of all international students – nearly half a million people (only slightly less than the United Kingdom). South Koreans are at present the largest single nationality studying in China. With large numbers of young people from other countries in the region, such as Thailand, Pakistan and India opting for Chinese universities – as well as growing numbers of Americans – this proportion may soon be changing.

Wine

The world's leading wine producing countries.

1.1m   39m

Hectolitres

Less   More

Italy
France
Spain

Imports   Leading producers

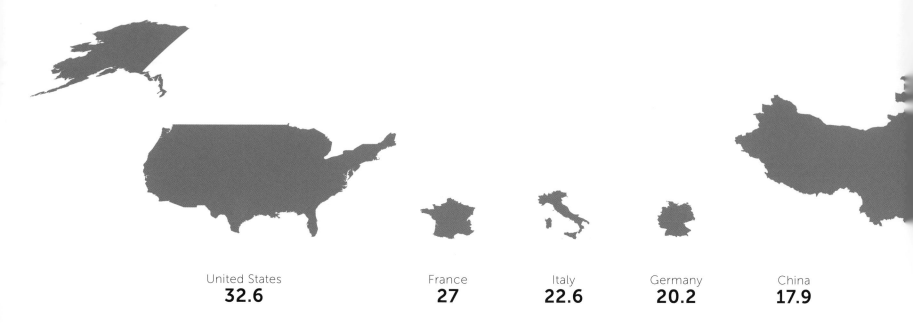

United States
32.6

France
27

Italy
22.6

Germany
20.2

China
17.9

Wine

Galileo reportedly called it 'sunlight, held together by water'. Benjamin Franklin claimed it made 'daily living easier, less hurried, with fewer tensions and more tolerance'. Robert Louis Stevenson described it as 'bottled poetry'. Ernest Hemingway argued it to be 'one of the most civilized things in the world'. Has any other beverage, or even any other product, ever conjured the consistent outpouring of love that wine manages to stimulate among the great and the good?

There are few consumables for which place of origin has quite the significance that it has for wine. Frequently, the desirability – and therefore the value – of a bottle of wine depends on where it is produced, right down to the precise region of a country, rather than its variety of grape or vintage. Major wines considered high value due to their particular 'appellations' include champagne, from northeastern France, port, from the Douro region of northern Portugal, and sherry, from the province of Jerez de la Frontera in Andalusia, Spain.

The world's top wine-producing countries are familiar names. Italy is the world's highest producer, with a total 50.9 million hectolitres in 2016 (1 hectolitre is equivalent to 100 litres/26 gallons). The next highest is France (43.5 million hectolitres), followed by Spain (39.3 million) and the United States (23.9 million). To a lesser volume, there are also significant quantities of wine being produced in 'New World' wine-growing regions, such as Australia, South Africa and Chile. The big European producers are also among the biggest drinkers, with the French, Italians and Spanish all consuming wine almost

United Kingdom
12.7

Spain
10.3

Russia
8.9

The leading global consumers of wine, in million hectolitres per year. France, Italy and Spain might be the world's premier wine producers, but no one consumes as much as the United States.

entirely from within their own borders, but still leaving plenty of produce left over for export. The United States is the world's top wine consumer, getting through 31 million hectolitres of wine every year. Two-thirds of this is sourced from the sun-drenched valleys of California – easily the country's biggest wine-producing state – while the rest is imported from either Australia or Italy, or to a lesser extent either Argentina or Chile.

Overall, the world consumes 240 million hectolitres of wine every year – enough to fill ten thousand Olympic-sized swimming pools. The United Kingdom is the sixth largest consumer, drinking nearly 13 million hectolitres annually. Being one of the few high-consuming countries that isn't also a major producer, this requires the United Kingdom to import around 14 million hectolitres every year, primarily from Italy and France, as well as, to a lesser extent, from New Zealand, Australia and Spain.

Making a surprise appearance as the world's sixth-largest producer of wine is China, with over 11 million hectolitres. Although there is archaeological evidence of wine cultivation in China many thousands of years ago, increased consumption is an extremely new development. The majority of China's vineyards are found in Xinjiang, in the northwest of the country, towards the border with Kazakhstan. China exports very little of its wine, but instead uses it to fuel its population's burgeoning demands. The love of wine that so enraptured the great minds of the past now extends to almost every corner of the planet.

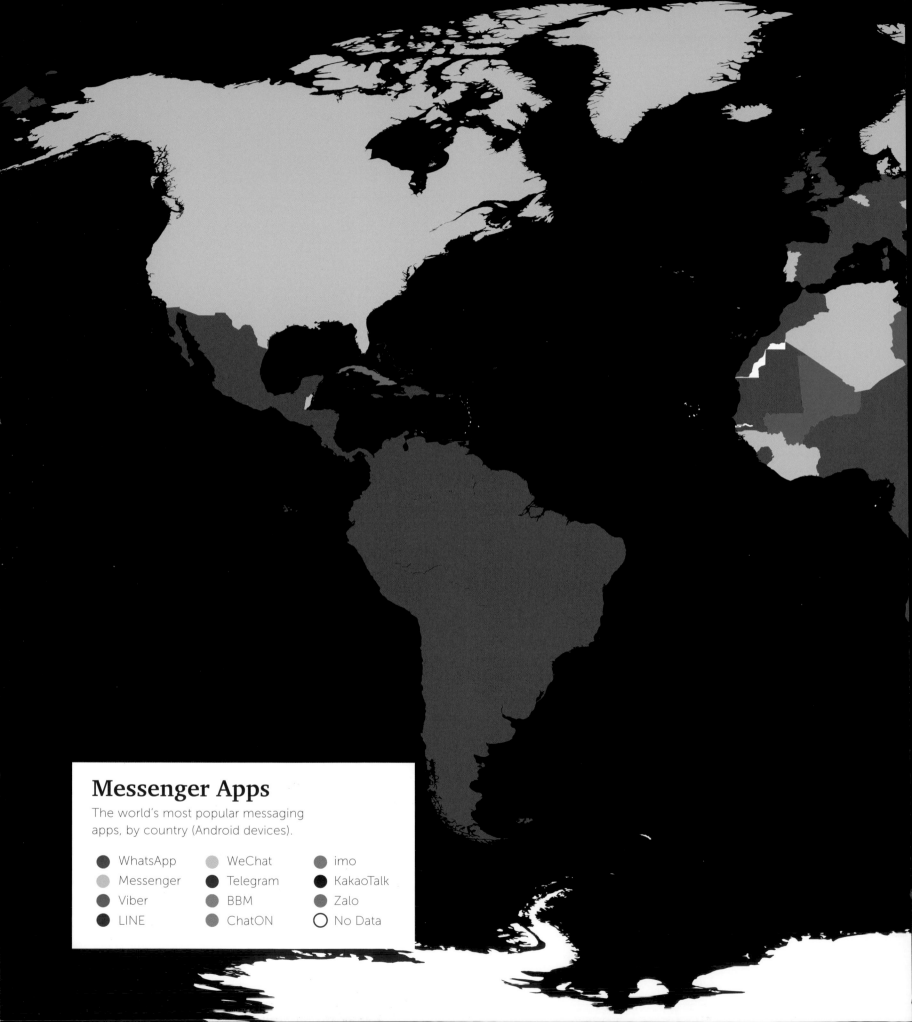

Messenger Apps

The world's most popular messaging apps, by country (Android devices).

- ● WhatsApp
- ● Messenger
- ● Viber
- ● LINE
- ● WeChat
- ● Telegram
- ● BBM
- ● ChatON
- ● imo
- ● KakaoTalk
- ● Zalo
- ○ No Data

Messenger Apps

Until he was sixteen years old, Jan Koum lived with his mother in a small village outside Kiev, Ukraine, in a house without electricity or running water, his father's construction work their only means of income. Following the collapse of the Soviet Union in 1991, the pair emigrated to Mountain View, California. While she babysat, he spent his high-school years sweeping floors and collecting food stamps to make ends meet, borrowing used books to teach himself how to code.

In the late 1990s, Koum began working at the internet company Yahoo, even dropping out of San José State University to focus on his career with the fledging internet giant. After he and fellow employee Brian Acton – a computer science graduate from Stanford – left the company in 2007, they were both turned down for a job at new social-media giant Facebook, and found themselves searching for a new project. After buying an Apple iPhone, Koum became intrigued by the possibilities offered by the new App Store that Apple was launching. In 2009, he and Acton founded an innovative new messaging app to share status updates between people in the phone's address book, software that gradually evolved to become an alternative to traditional text messaging. Five years later, they sold that app, WhatsApp, used by around 465 million people every month at the time, to rivals Facebook for a cool $19 billion. They signed the contract in the Mountain View social services building in which Koum used to claim his welfare cheques.

With more than 1.5 billion monthly users in December 2017, WhatsApp is now the world's biggest mobile messaging service, handling 65 billion messages per day. Despite the eye-watering price tag, WhatsApp does have fierce competition in the mobile messaging market. Facebook's own messaging app recorded 1.3 billion users in April 2018, while rivals such as WeChat and QQ – both extremely popular Chinese messaging systems – currently have 1 billion and 783 million users respectively. LINE, an alternative messaging app originally developed after telecommunication failures in the aftermath of the Japanese earthquake in March 2011, is particularly popular in Japan, Taiwan and Thailand, and has just over 200 million regular users.

Outside of China, where WhatsApp, like parent company Facebook, is banned, it is the most used messaging app in many different countries. In Turkey, around half the population are active WhatsApp users, a figure that rises to 56 per cent for both Brazil and Mexico; to 65 per cent for Germany; and 68 per cent for Malaysia. Perhaps the biggest fans of the app, however, are the Saudi Arabians, of whom nearly three-quarters are active users. It marks a dramatic change for the kingdom, where a longterm ban on VoIP (voice over internet) calls using the app was lifted in late 2017, part of a package of reforms to make the country more attractive to overseas businesses.

Today, across the large majority of the world, anyone with a smartphone and an internet connection is capable of sending messages to anyone else, across oceans and across borders. All WhatsApp messages are encrypted end-to-end by default, making them completely inaccessible by even WhatsApp staff. 'Technology is an amplifier,' Acton told *WIRED* magazine in 2016. 'With the right stewards in place, with the right guidance, we can really effect positive change.'

The number of monthly active WhatsApp users, in millions, worldwide from April 2013 to December 2017. WhatsApp usage has boomed to become the world's most popular messaging app.

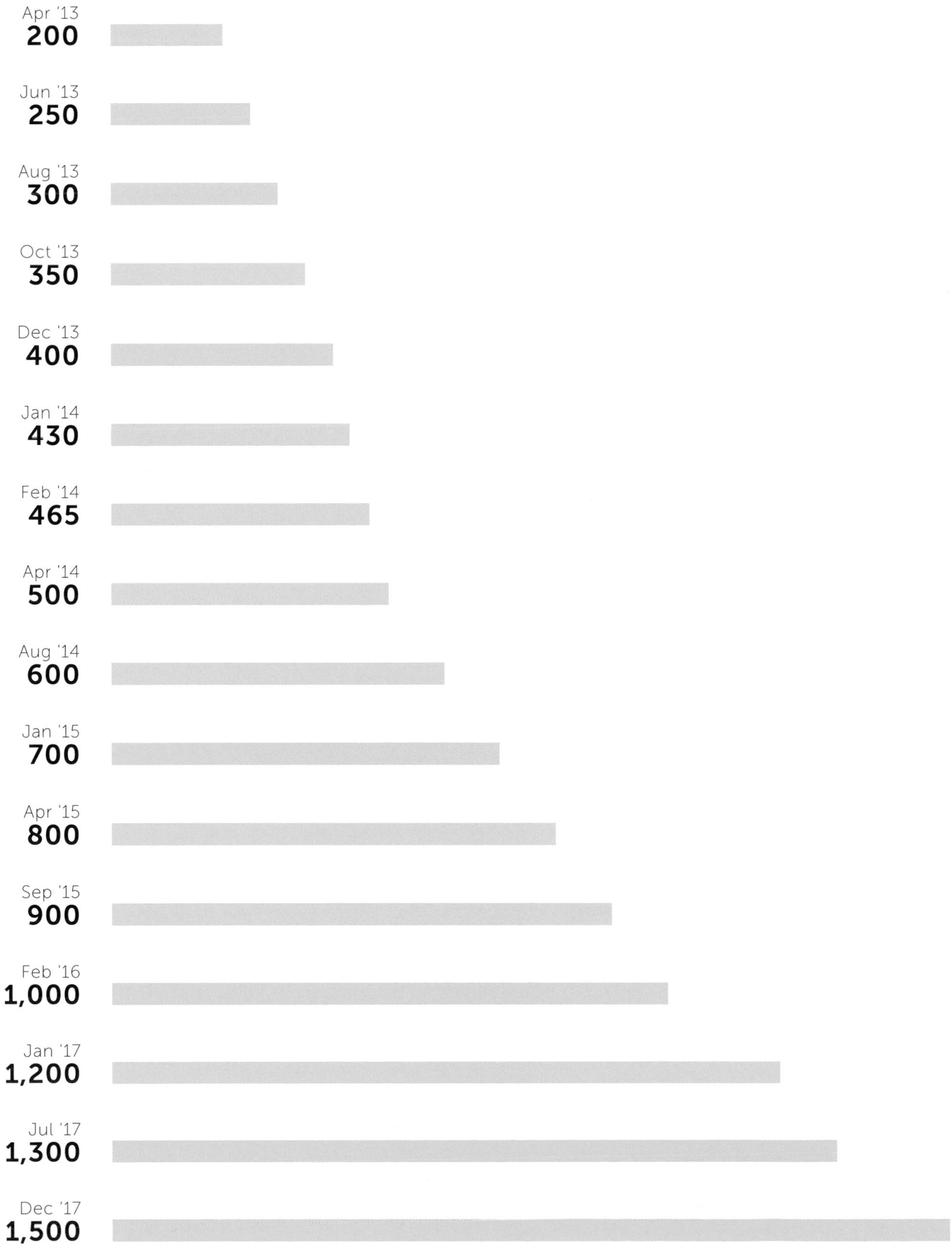

Apr '13
200

Jun '13
250

Aug '13
300

Oct '13
350

Dec '13
400

Jan '14
430

Feb '14
465

Apr '14
500

Aug '14
600

Jan '15
700

Apr '15
800

Sep '15
900

Feb '16
1,000

Jan '17
1,200

Jul '17
1,300

Dec '17
1,500

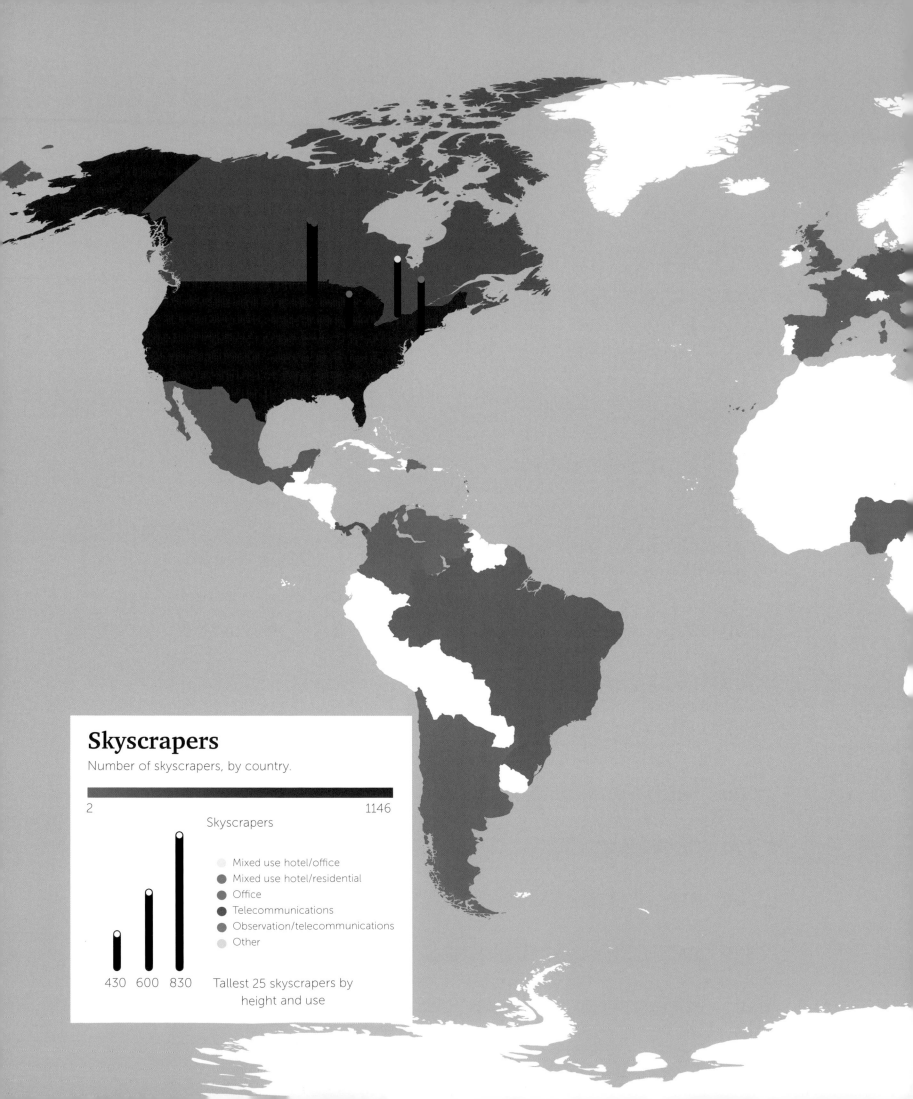

Skyscrapers

Number of skyscrapers, by country.

2   1146
Skyscrapers

○ Mixed use hotel/office
● Mixed use hotel/residential
● Office
● Telecommunications
● Observation/telecommunications
○ Other

430 600 830   Tallest 25 skyscrapers by
                  height and use

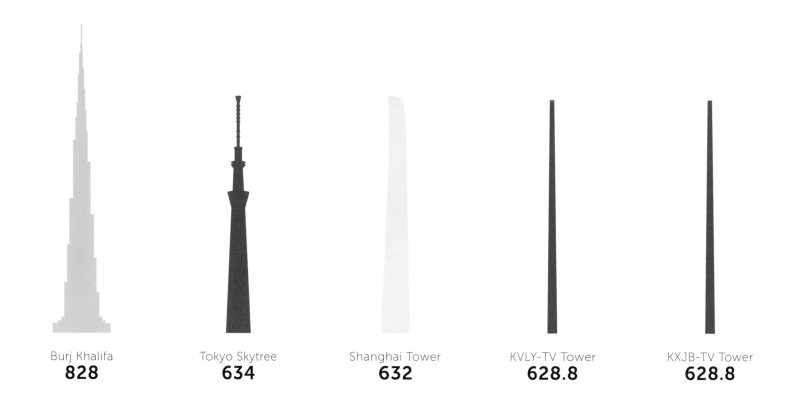

| Burj Khalifa | Tokyo Skytree | Shanghai Tower | KVLY-TV Tower | KXJB-TV Tower |
| **828** | **634** | **632** | **628.8** | **628.8** |

Skyscrapers

In 1311, the central tower of Lincoln Cathedral, in England's East Midlands, needed to be replaced. The new tower and accompanying spire made the cathedral the first human structure to measure more than 150m (492ft) tall. With its impressive new height of 160m (525ft), the cathedral surpassed the Great Pyramid of Giza as the tallest human structure in the world – a title it would hold for the next 238 years. Today, the United Kingdom has eighteen buildings that measure more than 150m (492ft) tall (Lincoln Cathedral no longer among them, since the collapse of its spire in 1549). While this figure may seem impressive the total is only one more than that of North Korea, and one less than those of both Israel and Colombia – numbers that are left in the shadows cast by those of other countries around the world.

In these days of reaching for the skies, no country is doing so more than China. At the time of writing, the country has a whopping 1,683 buildings measuring more than 150m (492ft) tall – more than double the number in the United States (741), the next highest. The only other countries with one hundred or more skyscrapers are Japan (241), the United Arab Emirates (228), South Korea (241) and Australia (100). Such structures have become a country's means of making its mark on the world stage, as witnessed by the battle for the title of 'world's tallest building'. Since the turn of the millennium, this has jumped from Kuala Lumpar's Petronas Towers (452m/1,483ft) to Taipei's Taipei 101 (508m/1,667ft) to Dubai's Burj Khalifa (828m/2,717ft). Even this last mega structure will likely be usurped soon, by Saudi Arabia's Jeddah

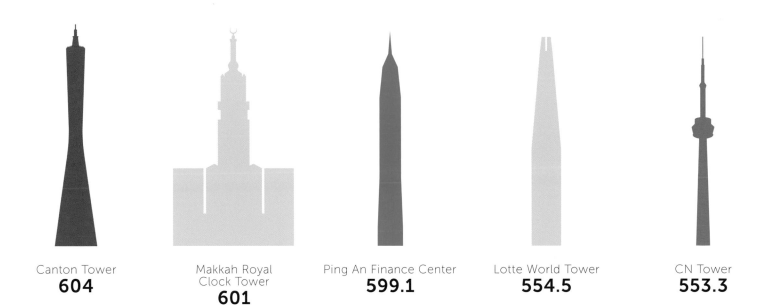

Canton Tower
604

Makkah Royal
Clock Tower
601

Ping An Finance Center
599.1

Lotte World Tower
554.5

CN Tower
553.3

The world's 10 tallest
buildings, in metres

Tower, which will reach an incredible 1,000m (3,281ft) – one entire kilometre – into the sky when finished. It's particularly striking that America – site of the birth of the skyscraper – now has no buildings in the world's top-ten, the tallest being New York's One World Trade Center, at 541m/1,775ft. The rate of new scrapers is escalating quickly; whereas the year 2000 saw just seventy-eight new buildings over 150m (492ft) tall being constructed worldwide, in 2017 there were an incredible 296 new buildings, a trend that looks set to continue to grow as the world's population urbanizes.

Seemingly the most obvious reason for building a skyscraper might be in order to fit more valuable floor space into a limited area. While there is undoubtedly value to making a city more dense, and therefore limiting the sprawl at the outer edges, the world's tallest skyscrapers are also increasingly a way for rich and booming cities to show off, make a statement and put themselves firmly on the global map. The very concept of the skyscraper has transcended cultures to become recognized globally as a symbol of capitalism. Thanks to the globalization of urban architecture, the skylines of the world's cities are becoming increasingly similar. Overwhelmingly, whether situated in Seoul or Chicago, Dubai or Guangzhou, the use of these buildings as high-flying apartments, office blocks and hotels stands testimony to how successfully the iconic multipurpose skyscrapers first launched in Manhattan around the turn of the twentieth century have since taken over the world.

Copper

Largest export quantities from Chile, the leading global producer of copper.

Less   More

620k   5.5m

Tonnes

Copper

In October 2010, the world watched transfixed as, in a remote corner of Chile's Atacama Desert, a strange capsule emerged from a hole in the ground. A hatch opened, and a man staggered out. His name was Florencio Avalos. Thirty-one years old, his clothes were dirty, and he wore sunglasses to protect his eyes from the bright spotlights all around. Against all the odds, he was alive, for Avalos had just spent two months trapped underground, ever since the San José mine he had been working in had suffered a severe collapse, trapping him and his thirty-two colleagues nearly 800m (½ mile) below ground. One-by-one, each miner was carefully winched to the surface to be reunited with his loved ones. By some miracle, all thirty-three men survived.

The men had been mining for copper, the reddish base metal that helps power most of the modern world. The San José mine was operated at the time by San Esteban, one of a number of private firms that work alongside the state *Corporación Nacional del Cobre de Chile* (Codelco), the world's largest producer of copper. The copper industry forms the backbone of the Chilean economy, contributing as much as 20 per cent of the national GDP, and upwards of 60 per cent of all national exports.

The extent to which the rest of the world relies on Chile for copper is quite remarkable. The country is known to have at least 170 million tonnes in reserves, comfortably more than the next highest countries, Australia (88 million) and Peru (81 million). In 2016, more than one-third of all copper mined from the ground worldwide was derived from Chile – around 5.5 million tonnes, more than two hundred times the weight of New York's Statue of Liberty (which happens to be plated in copper, hence its green hue). Raw copper is shipped to countries such as China, Japan, South Korea, India, and the United States, where, thanks to its high electrical conductivity, it plays a vital role in the twenty-first century's technological revolution. It is especially important in ubiquitous electric power cables, telephone cables and computer circuit boards.

The versatility and multiple application of copper has seen global consumption steadily climb over the past decade, from less than 17 million tonnes in 2006, to nearly 24 million by 2016. While experts are divided on

Building
construction
43%

Transportation
equipment
19%

Electric and
electronic
products
19%

Consumer
and general
products
12%

Industrial
machinery
and
equipment
7%

Of the wide variety of uses
for copper and copper
alloy products in the
United States, construction
consumes nearly half of
the metal.

whether the world will ever face 'peak copper', this growing demand saw the
metal's price peak at nearly $9,000 per tonne in 2011, before gradually
declining to just over $6,000 by 2017. Since copper has been ever-present in
electrical cabling for nearly two centuries, the market for second-hand copper
has boomed as the price has risen, with treasure hunters scouring scrap-metal
dumps in search of the valuable material – in the most extreme cases cables
have even been ripped out of the ground. In 2015, the global production of
refined secondary copper topped 3.9 million tonnes, almost double
production just one decade earlier. The rarer copper becomes, and the more
the world demands it, the more pressure Chile will find itself under to meet
that demand.

Patents: International

Total number of patent applications, by country.

| 1 | 1k | 10k | 100k | 1m | 1.2m |

No data

100%
70%
0%

Percentage of nation's patent
applications registered internationally

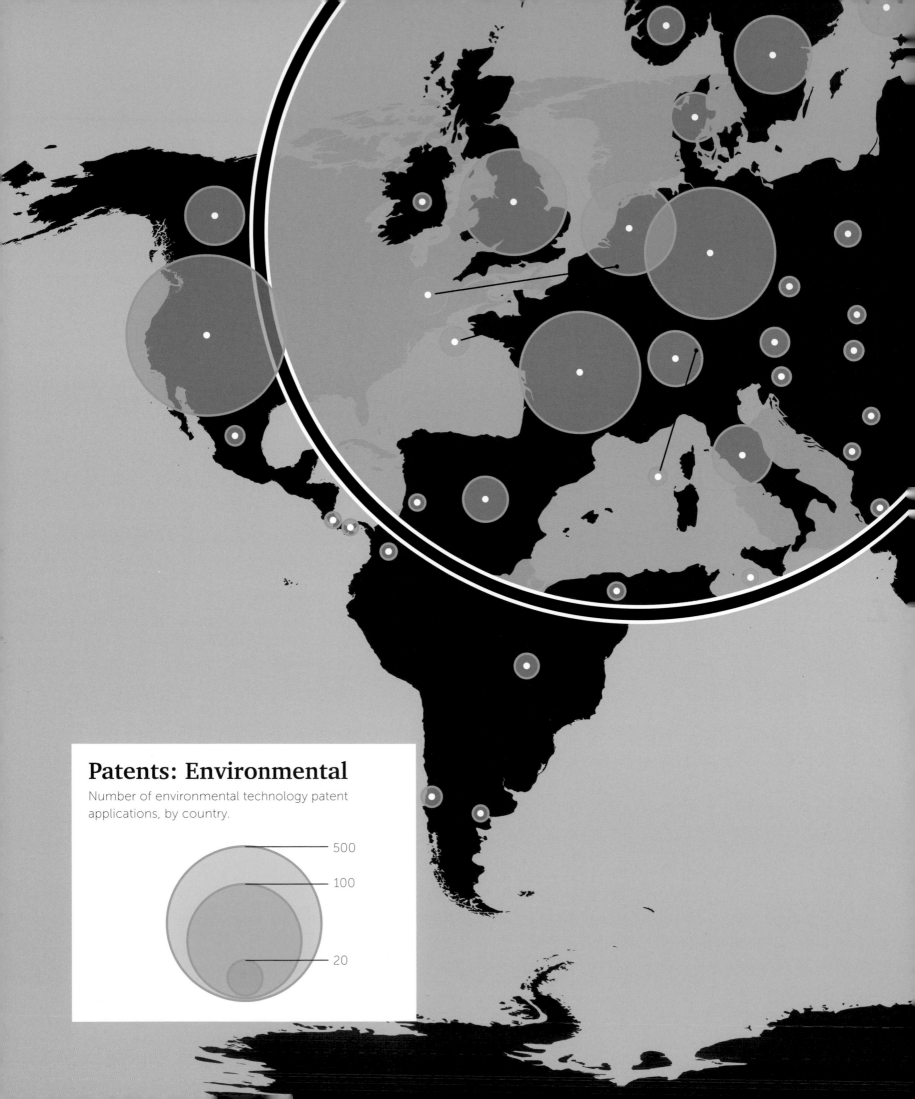

Patents: Environmental

Number of environmental technology patent applications, by country.

500

100

20

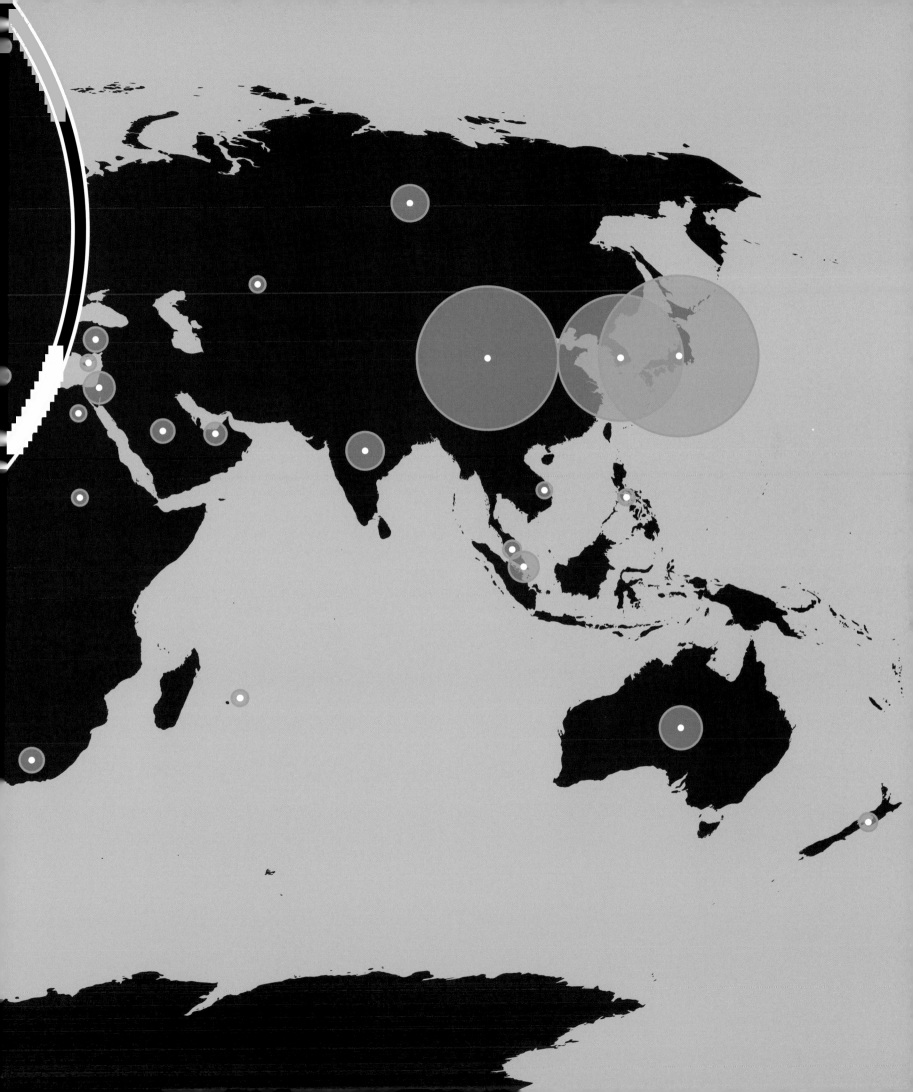

Patents

A casual glance at the latest technology news will reveal that securing a patent has become a prerequisite for launching an innovative new product. A successful patent application will protect the intellectual property of whoever devised a new product against rivals mimicking or simply ripping off their idea – even if the orginator doesn't subsequently create the item in question. Payouts of tens, even hundreds, of millions of dollars are not unknown in this respect. Popular new products can sell in their millions, and so with potentially huge profits on the line, it is in the interest of major companies to file as many patent applications as they possibly can, in the hope of gaining a noteworthy advantage over rivals in the race for consumers' attention.

In 2016, the China national patent office received a total of 1.34 million patents applications – the highest number by any single country in the world (over 404,000 were granted). Ninety per cent of these applications came from domestic companies and organizations, showing how relatively few foreign companies are trying to sell into China, compared to local companies – by comparison, only half of the patent applications made in the United States during the same period came from within America, evidence of overseas companies wishing to sell their products into the United States. The Chinese figure represents exceptionally rapid growth, especially in the country's high-tech industry (2006 saw 24,301 patent applications in this field, rising to 131,680 by 2016). The US and China are also among the largest applicants for environmental technology patents, with 536 and 356 respectively. Only Japan applied for more, with 546 applications.

In total, China has 1.77 million patents currently active – that is, those already granted but not yet expired. The United States may have more active patents than any other nation – 2.76 million, with Japan the next highest, at 1.98 million – but with just 600,000 applications made, Americans sought less than half the number of patents in 2016, than China did. Overall, the global number of patents applied for has rapidly climbed year by year, from 997,501 in 1990 (406,582 granted) to 3,127,900 in 2016 (1,651,600 granted).

One key rule of patents is that each national patent office only has the power to grant a patent to cover the territory in which they are filed, meaning that it is necessary for companies to apply for a patent for the same product over and over again in different countries. One alternative is to apply for a Patent Cooperation Treaty (PCT), a concept first launched in the late 1970s. Administered by the World Intellectual Property Organisation (WIPO), this is the closest thing there is to an international patent, recognizing intellectual

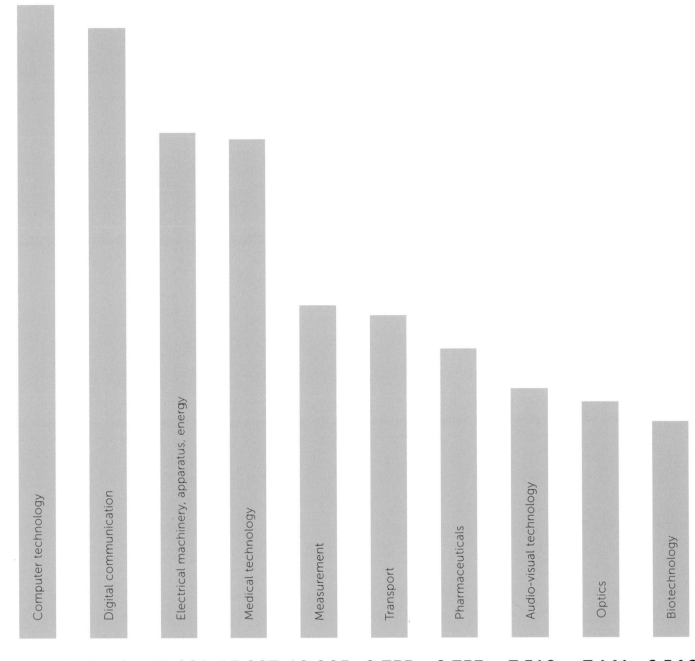

19,123	18,401	15,225	15,027	10,085	9,755	8,753	7,518	7,141	6,546

Computer technology · Digital communication · Electrical machinery, apparatus, energy · Medical technology · Measurement · Transport · Pharmaceuticals · Audio-visual technology · Optics · Biotechnology

Tens of thousands of PCT patents are registered every year, overwhelmingly in digital technology.

property across over 150 territories from a single patent application. Smartphone manufacturer Huawei applied for 4,024 PCT patents in 2017, the most by any company in the world, followed by 2,965 PCTs applied for by another Chinese company, ZTE Corporation, an indication that they aspire to have the next big thing overseas. Overall, there were 48,882 PCT patent applications from China in 2017, slightly more than those from Japan (48,208), but still far fewer than those from the United States (59,624). The battle for ideas continues to heat up.

Vanilla

The world's vanilla producing countries.

10   2,900

Tonnes

Canada
2.70%

Netherland
3.80%

Belgium ————
2.10%

USA
39%

France
23%

Vanilla

It may be the most basic of all ice-cream flavours, but there's more to vanilla
than meets the taste bud. Vanilla is a globally desired commodity, an essential
ingredient in a wide assortment of flavoured food and fragrances, and more
expensive than many rival spices due to the time-consuming and highly
labour-intensive method of growing and processing vanilla beans. But its
surging popularity is causing major social and environmental problems in
some corners of the world.

While there are several varieties of suitable plants, the vast majority of
commercial vanilla comes from one specific species, a variety of orchid –
Vanilla planifolia. Believed to be first cultivated by Mexican Aztecs, this yellow-
flowered plant grows as a thick vine that can be up to 30m (98ft) in length. It
produces long, thin, pod-like fruits packed with thousands of tiny seeds. At
this stage the pods have no particular flavour, but are harvested, cured and
dried over several weeks or months to produce a valuable and distinctive
spice. Traditionally it was used to flavour cocoa.

Vanilla first went global in the sixteenth century, when Spanish explorers
brought it back to Europe from Mexico. Three centuries later, the French
introduced the crop to their Indian Ocean colonies of Réunion Island,
Comoros and the large island of Madagascar. Madagascar, in particular,
embraced the opportunity to grow and sell this new commodity, and by
the present day has become the world's leading supplier of vanilla. In 2016,
2,926 tonnes – the weight of around 500 adult elephants – were produced
on the island, ahead of Indonesia (2,304 tonnes), China (885 tonnes), Mexico
(513 tonnes) and Papua New Guinea (502 tonnes). These raw spices are

Germany
17%

Switzerland
1.20%

Japan
2.00%

India
1.00%

Mauritius
5.70%

The 10 leading importers of Madagascan vanilla, by percentage of total exports. It travels all around the world, but more than a third is shipped straight to the United States.

primarily exported to the United States ($210 million worth), France ($125 million) and Germany ($94 million), Madagascar's three key vanilla customers, ahead of the $31 million exported to Indian Ocean neighbours Mauritius. Commercially, vanilla is used to flavour everything from cakes to perfumes and soft drinks as well as ice cream. It is also added to other sweet treats to enhance the flavour of other ingredients, such as coffee, chocolate and caramel.

In recent years, prices have surged due to a lack of supply resulting from poor harvests, often owing to extreme weather events. The trend has been a blow for ice-cream manufacturers and perfumeries, but an economic boom for small-scale Madagascan vanilla farmers, whose harvests are suddenly worth up to ten times what they were only a few years previously. The desire to profit from the high prices has seen rapid and relentless deforestation across the Indian Ocean island, as land is cleared to create more space for planting the profitable crop. Victims of this activity include Madagascar's iconic ring-tailed lemur, currently classified as 'endangered'.

The fact that vanilla production is a labour-intensive process, coupled with the volatility of global supply, has spawned renewed interest in synthetic vanilla, a practice first attempted as long ago as 1874 from pine bark and, later, from cloves. For manufacturers wanting to capture the 'essence' of this aromatic spice without paying top dollar for the real thing, synthetic flavourings derived from wood pulp and coal-tar are now commercially available. It's just one more factor that contributes to the tensions and uncertainty that surround the future of authentic vanilla, still one of the world's most popular flavours.

VANILLA

Cobalt

Leading countries by percentage of total global cobalt production.

0.6%   58.8%

— 280k
— 150k °
— 30k

Sized by total cobalt reserves, tonnes

DRC
3.5m

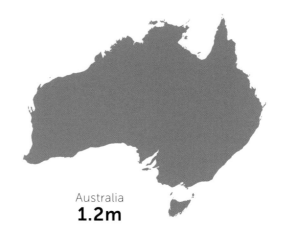

Australia
1.2m

Cobalt

Deep in the remote Congo rainforest, amid the lush, green vegetation, thousands of weary arms toil in the hot and humid environment for at least twelve, but sometimes as many as twenty-four hours a day. The arms belong to miners, who use hand tools to plough deep tunnels into the ground. Collectively known as 'creuseurs', from the French, meaning 'diggers', these miners, many of them children, burrow into the hillside. They are scavenging for the discarded by-products of industrial mines such as copper and nickel, and specifically for dark stones with a navy-blue hue – the ore of a metal that is becoming increasingly essential for powering much of the modern world: cobalt.

The more we fill our lives with electronic devices, from smartphones and laptops to e-readers and electric cars, the more the world becomes dependent on lithium ion batteries. Their manufacture relies on a regular supply of metals, particularly cobalt and nickel, and demands for these metals are highly likely to rise. Even just from 2016 to 2018, the price of cobalt quadrupled, driven primarily by the boom in electric cars.

The world's supply of cobalt is concentrated in only a few regions of the world, placing significant pressure upon local producers. Just over half of the world's cobalt supply currently comes from the Democratic Republic of the Congo (DRC), more than ten times more than any other country (far smaller quantities also emanate from such countries as China, Canada, Russia and Australia). The DRC has the world's largest reserves of unmined cobalt,

Cuba
500k

Philippines
280k

Zambia
270k

at 3.5 million tonnes, considerably more than Australia, with the second highest of 1.2 million.

While the DRC's mining industry creates employment in a country where poverty is rife, a lack of adequate equipment coupled with poor environmental standards means that working conditions are poor at best. Hazards are manifold and fatal accidents, such as tunnel collapses, common. Furthermore, increasing demand for the supply of cobalt ore has resulted in a large number of unregulated mines across the DRC, supplying as much as 20 per cent of the country's total cobalt exports in 2016.

Once mined, cobalt ore is transported to various domestic markets, where traders test, buy and collect the ore. The daily prices for the ore are displayed on handwritten notes, and often no questions are asked about where the minerals have come from. It is then processed and smelted by companies such as Congo Dongfang Mining International, before being exported via Kinshasa to countries such as China and South Korea, where many of the world's lithium ion batteries are now manufactured. The 60 per cent of cobalt that doesn't eventually become a battery of some kind is likely to be used for tyres (4 per cent), magnets (5 per cent), steel (7 per cent), diamond drills (10 per cent) or superalloys (16 per cent). Whatever the end use, it's a long journey from deep below ground in the Congo rainforest to the global supply chain.

The 5 countries with the largest cobalt reserves, in tonnes, led by the remote forests of the DRC.

COBALT

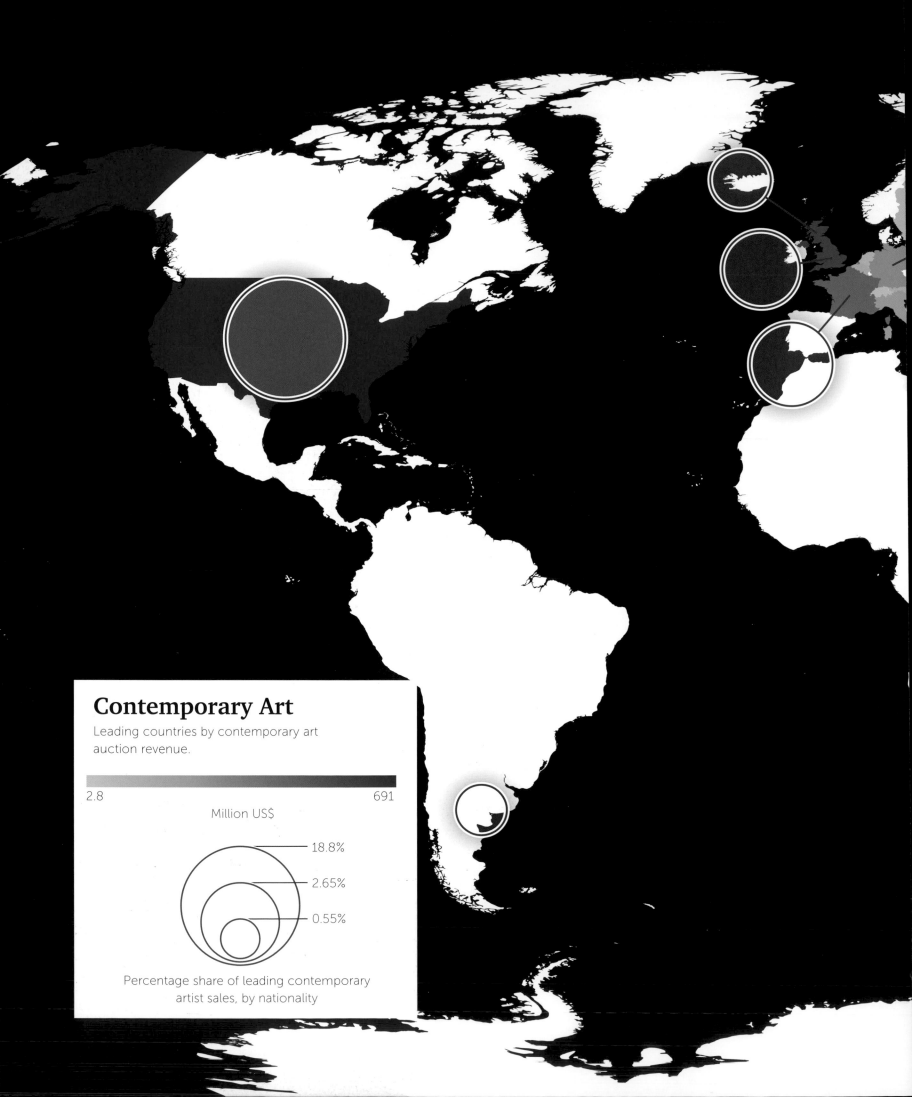

Contemporary Art

Leading countries by contemporary art auction revenue.

2.8   691

Million US$

18.8%

2.65%

0.55%

Percentage share of leading contemporary artist sales, by nationality

Jean-Michel Basquiat
5.4%

Andy Warhol
4.4%

Cy Twombly
2.7%

Contemporary Art

Jean-Michel Basquiat was a self-taught artist who grew up in Brooklyn, New York, in the 1960s and 1970s. After dropping out of high school, and moving out of home aged seventeen, he lived on the streets, or squatted in abandoned buildings. During this time, he developed a passion for graffiti, adopting a raw, haphazardly colourful style that mixed influences from a variety of cultures, including his own Caribbean heritage (his parents hailed from Puerto Rico, where Basquiat spent some of his teenage years). The 1980s saw him participate in numerous high-profile exhibitions, and ultimately obtain a celebrity lifestyle – befriending famous pop artist Andy Warhol – until his untimely death in 1988, aged just twenty-seven.

One of his artworks, a large untitled canvas made in 1982 was bought in May 1984 for $20,900. Thirty-three years later, in May 2017, the hammer came down at an auction at Sotheby's, New York, securing a record-breaking price of $110.5 million for that same artwork – to Japanese collector and technology entrepreneur Yusaku Maezawa – making it easily the most expensive piece of contemporary art to date.

It was the standout sale in a year in which New York showed itself to be one of the dominant centres of the contemporary art market – that is, works by artists operating in the present era, sometimes loosely determined as those born since 1945. All of the top five contemporary art sales in 2016–2017 occurred in New York, and total sales amounted to $690.5 million, meaning the United States accounted for nearly half of global contemporary art turnover. The United States' domination is underlined by the growing gulf between it and the two other major contemporary art markets, China

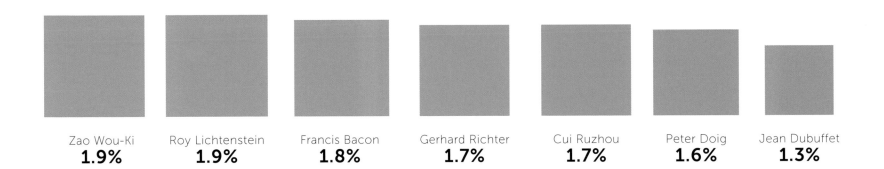

Zao Wou-Ki	Roy Lichtenstein	Francis Bacon	Gerhard Richter	Cui Ruzhou	Peter Doig	Jean Dubuffet
1.9%	**1.9%**	**1.8%**	**1.7%**	**1.7%**	**1.6%**	**1.3%**

Americans dominate the most commercially successful contemporary art charts, led by New York artist Jean-Michel Basquiat. Figures show % of 2017 contemporary art sales.

($369.6 million) and the United Kingdom ($348.4 million). Overall, New York, London, Hong Kong and Beijing now collectively account for more than 80 per cent of all contemporary art auction turnover.

China's contemporary art market, in particular, is undergoing something of a revolution, especially with wealthy buyers turning their attention towards historic masterpieces. Enormous sums of money have been spent in recent years to bring classics such as those by Monet and Van Gogh to Chinese collectors, leaving less money available for contemporary works. Nevertheless, Chinese contemporary artists comprised 162 of the top 500 places when ranked by the volume of money taken at auction in 2016–17, ahead of 139 European artists and only 97 Americans. Works that perform particularly well among domestic buyers in Chinese auctions are ink paintings evoking traditional Chinese imagery. There is also growing interest in contemporary art by artists of African origin. Recent high-profile exhibitions in Paris have sought out fresh talent in the African art scene, such as Nigerian Njideka Akunyili Crosby, who was the biggest-selling African artist in 2016–17, at over $10 million. The emergence of Crosby and contemporaries runs parallel with new buyers in Johannesburg, Cape Town and Lagos looking for new artworks from the continent. However, these cities would have to sell a lot of artworks to dream of competing with the contemporary art powerhouses of Hong Kong, London or New York.

Cinema

Revenue of the world's 10 leading box office markets.

0.2   10.3

Billion US$

2,000

1,000

200

Sized by number of films produced

200

283

254

789

Cinema

Whether involving science-fiction stories set in outer space, children's animations with talking animals and robots or the adventures of big-name superheroes, the tens of billions of dollars taken at cinema box offices worldwide is an illustration of the power of the movie industry. It also highlights the supremely dominant role Hollywood enjoys globally – as illustrated by the attention paid annually to the Academy Awards 'Oscars' ceremony.

There is no more dominant source of movies than the United States, with the highest-grossing films worldwide coming out of American studios, focused around globally recognizable franchises such as Star Wars and the Marvel Universe, or children's animations by Pixar and DreamWorks. However, although Hollywood released 789 movies in 2016, more than Japan (610), France (283) and the United Kingdom (200), and nearly as many as China (944), the undisputed number one in pure quantity remains India, with Bollywood churning out a remarkable 1,903 feature films annually (nearly double the number from ten years ago).

Although they might not be household names outside of India, Bollywood actors such as Shah Rukh Khan, Salman Khan and Akshay Kumar were all among the top ten highest paid actors in the world in 2017. With the rapid expansion of multiplex cinemas – there are now over 2,000 across India – and nearly 2 billion tickets sold in 2017 (compared to 1.1 billion in the US and 1.6 billion in China in the same year), Bollywood is big business. The overseas market is growing just as fast, and is expected to double in revenue by 2021 to

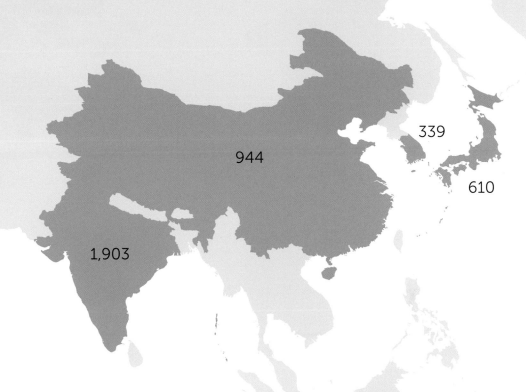

224

339

944

610

1,903

over 15 billion rupees ($230 million). With these numbers, Mumbai might even claim to be able to compete with Hollywood for the title of 'movie capital of the world'.

Nevertheless, North America remains the number-one market worldwide for recouping the millions spent on big-budget blockbusters, earning $10.2 billion in 2017, followed by China (earning $8.4 billion), then Japan ($2.2 billion), the United Kingdom ($1.7 billion) and India ($1.5 billion). Chinese box offices are becoming so profitable – growing by up to 30 per cent annually – that Hollywood studios are increasingly catering specifically to these audiences; the version of the 2013 Marvel hit *Iron Man 3* that screened in China included an extra eight-minute scene featuring famous Chinese actors.

Despite the rise of new technologies with the potential to beam hits from the silver screen directly into our homes, and even the decision by many distributors to bypass theatrical releases entirely, visiting the cinema remains as popular as ever. Globally, ticket sales rose from eight billion in 2014, to nearly nine billion in 2018. Thanks to rising ticket prices, and these new global audiences, it also remains increasingly profitable, with global box-office revenues growing from $23 billion in 2005 to $40 billion in 2017, and an anticipated nearly $50 billion by 2020. Critics have been prepared to declare the death of the cinema for decades, but all the evidence instead points towards a new golden age, and on a truly global scale.

International cinemas might be dominated by big budget movies from Hollywood, but their Bollywood rivals in India produce over twice as many films each year.

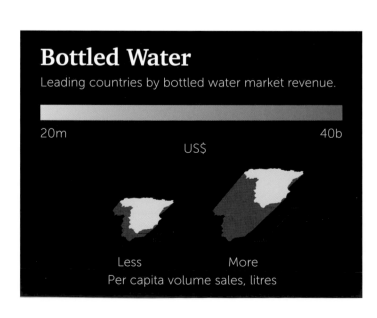

Bottled Water

Leading countries by bottled water market revenue.

20m   40b

US$

Less   More

Per capita volume sales, litres

Bottled Water

Since first coming into existence in seventeenth-century English spas as a special health cure, the popularity of mineral water has soared. Global consumption of bottled water nearly doubled in just ten years – from 212 billion litres (56 gallons) annually in 2007, to in excess of 391 billion litres (103 gallons) in 2017. While the large populations of China, India and the United States consume the greatest volume of bottled water, the most interesting trends can be found in the per capita figures, where Mexico, Thailand and Italy lead the way.

Mexico, for example, has shot up the bottled water consumption rankings, partly thanks to the introduction of the country's first 'soda tax' in January 2014, an attempt to tackle the escalating health and obesity crisis in a country where more than 70 per cent of the population is overweight, and over 30 per cent obese. Ongoing concerns about the cleanliness of tap water following a cholera outbreak in Mexico City after its 1985 earthquake have seen people willing to pay to ensure a clean supply of water, with stories of bottled water being used to bathe babies.

Often high consumption of bottled water emerges from ingrained cultural habits and an awareness of the status symbol that drinking expensive bottled water can project, but also from a concern regarding hygiene. In Thailand, for example, contamination of tap water means bottled water is even used for brushing teeth, which explains why the country is the second highest consumer, behind Mexico. In Spain and Italy, it is entirely safe to drink the tap water, yet habits of a lifetime persist, with many families opting for bottles as a guarantee of safety. In many Middle Eastern countries, such as Saudi Arabia or the United Arab Emirates, the majority of the tap-water supply is derived from desalinated seawater, a fact that encourages the country's newly wealthy consumers to continue their purchases of bottled water.

Bottled water has caused controversy in some parts of the world where bottling plants sit alongside poor communities suffering from water shortages. Further environmental issues emerge when considering the extraordinary volume of plastic waste created. With so much plastic currently being dumped into the ocean every year, it is predicted that by 2050 there will be more plastic in the ocean than fish. Plastic bottles are a major component of this, alongside plastic carrier bags and plastic straws.

The planet's thirst for bottled water therefore raises major challenges on a global scale. Many cities and countries are – through a focus on plastic taxes, reusable bottles and free water fountains – finally beginning the long process of tackling these problems. However, since 844 million people globally lack even a basic drinking-water source, the future of bottled water will likely depend on whether emerging nations can respond to the growing demands of their citizens and provide a constant source of clean, drinkable tap water. If not, then bottled water is most certainly here to stay.

The 10 largest per capita consumers of bottled water, in gallons during a year.

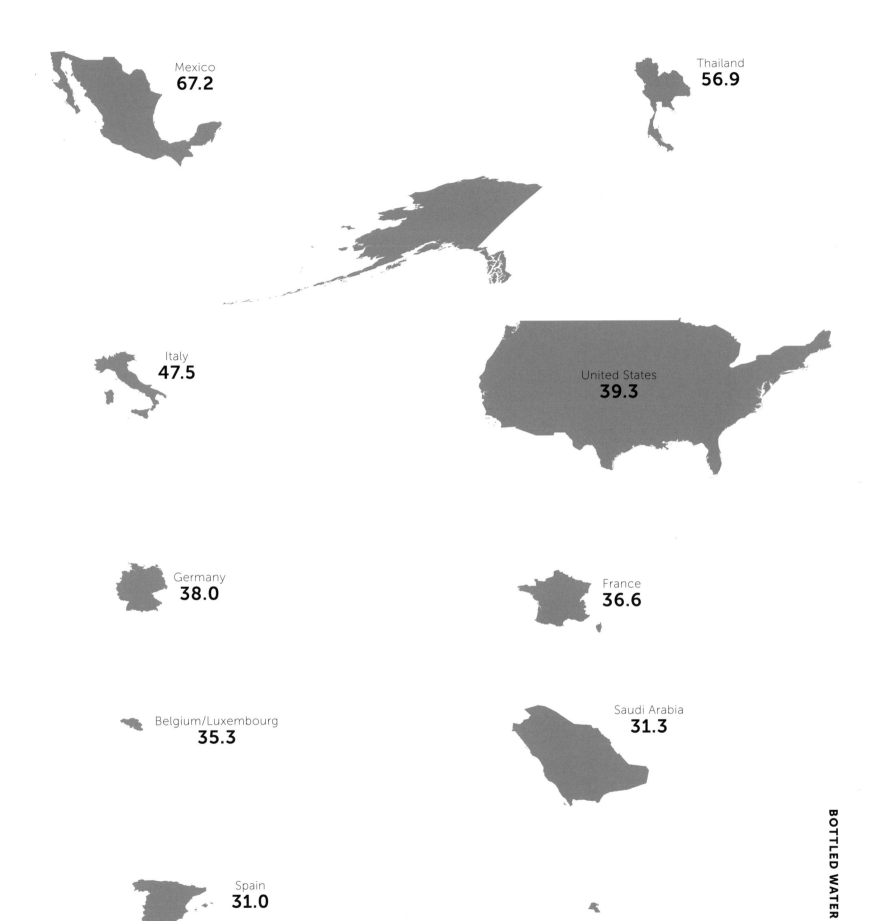

Mexico
67.2

Thailand
56.9

Italy
47.5

United States
39.3

Germany
38.0

France
36.6

Belgium/Luxembourg
35.3

Saudi Arabia
31.3

Spain
31.0

United Arab Emirates
30.7

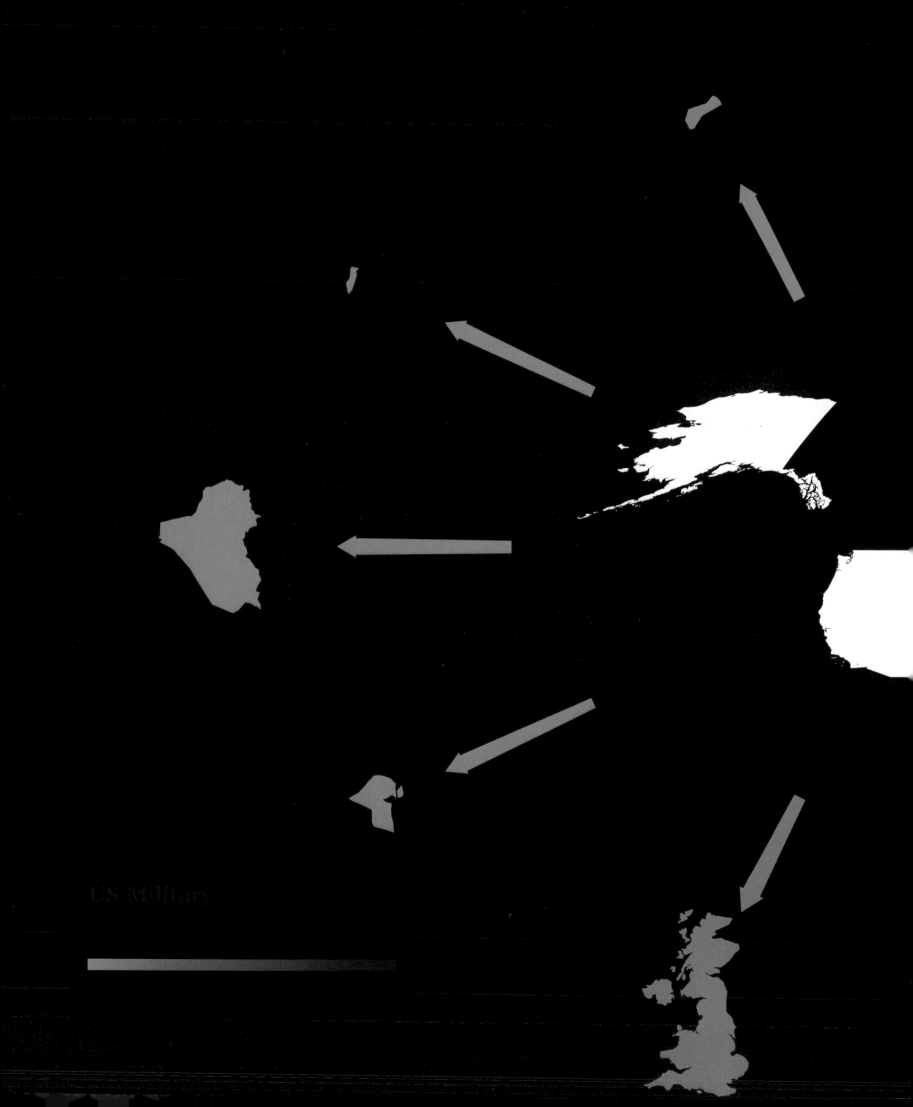

US Military

United Kingdom
8,500

Germany
34,800

Italy
12,100

Iraq
5,500

Afghanistan
9,300

Kuwait
6,300

Bahrain
5,500

US Military

Globally, the turn of the millennium coincided with a boom in military spending. From just over $1 trillion in 2001, the collective amount spent by all nations on troops, planes, tanks, rockets and other firepower had soared to nearly $1.7 trillion by 2016.

Military spending in the United States completely dwarfs every other country on Earth, reaching over $600 billion in 2017 – a fall from the $700 billion peak of 2011, but expected to rise over the coming decade. The United States therefore spent more than one-third of global military spending; in comparison, China's outlay (the world's second highest) was a mere $228 billion, followed by Saudi Arabia ($69 billion), Russia ($66 billion), India ($64 billion) and France ($58 billion).

Aside from the vast funds that are pumped into it, what really makes the US military stand out is the large number of bases overseas. The current US military consists of more than 2.1 million soldiers, nearly 200,000 of whom are deployed in active service overseas. Including family members, this means that around half a million Americans are being hosted overseas for the purpose of national defence.

Prior to the 1940s, the United States had almost no overseas presence, a situation that changed dramatically during and in the aftermath of the Second World War, with most troops based in the territories of defeated opponents; in 2016 there were 39,300 American military personnel based in Japan, and 34,800 in Germany. An additional 23,500 are kept on permanent standby in South Korea (more than sixty years since the armistice that brought the

South Korea
23,500

Japan
39,300

Guam
3,800

Korean War to an end) and, more recently, bases in the Middle East have witnessed the deployment of 5,500 American troops in Iraq, with another 5,500 stationed in Bahrain and 6,300 in Kuwait. Bases can also be found in other geographically strategic countries, including Australia (for the South Pacific), Colombia (for Central and South America, as well as the Caribbean) and Bulgaria (for Eastern Europe and the rest of Eurasia), totalling around 800 in no fewer than 30 countries around the world.

In contrast, China (the world's second-highest military spender) has no official overseas military bases, though they have a number of outposts in the South China Sea, including the Spratly Islands. Fellow UN Security Council members such as the United Kingdom, France and Russia have only a handful of bases, predominantly left over from their respective former colonies. 'Although few US citizens realise it, we probably have more bases in other people's lands than any other people, nation, or empire in world history,' writes author and academic David Vine, in his 2015 book *Base Nation*. Outlining how prevalent such bases are, he claims that, for many people around the world living nearby, they are 'one of the most prominent symbols of the United States, along with Hollywood movies, pop music, and fast food.'

Japan has the highest US military presence, closely followed by Germany. Figures show the number of military personnel based in each country, excluding civilian employees.

Cocoa

The world's leading producers of cocoa beans and per capita the highest consumers of chocolate, by country.

11.6k	1.47m

Cocoa production, tonnes

0.1	8.8

Chocolate consumption per capita, kilograms

Switzerland	Austria	Germany	Ireland	Great Britain
8.8	**8.1**	**7.9**	**7.9**	**7.6**

Cocoa

There's a particular type of tree native to the Americas that produces a quite distinctive variety of bean – one that, for three thousand years, indigenous people such as the Aztecs brewed to make a nutritious drink. The tree's Latin name is *Theobroma cacao*, although it is more commonly known as cocoa, the source of the world's most popular sweet treat: chocolate.

Despite its traditional roots, in the twenty-first century more than three-quarters of the world's total agricultural cocoa – which currently stands at 4 million tonnes – is grown on the other side of the Atlantic, in Africa. The crop only grows within 20° either north or south of the equator. Falling within this range is the Ivory Coast, which produced comfortably the largest quantities of cocoa in the world in 2017, a massive 1.8 million tonnes, twice as much as West African neighbour Ghana. The Netherlands is the primary destination for exported cocoa shipped from the Ivory Coast, the Dutch being the world's leading processors of cocoa beans (more than half a million tonnes annually). Lesser quantities of cocoa are also grown in Indonesia, Ecuador, Cameroon, Nigeria, Brazil and Papua New Guinea.

The Ivory Coast's intimate relationship with growing cocoa originates from the 1960s and 1970s, when millions of people began clearing themselves small plots of land in the forested interior of the country to begin their very own cocoa farms. Today, the beans are still sourced primarily from small-scale producers – here, and in most other cocoa-growing countries. Crucially, it is only in recent years that the Ivory Coast has begun processing its own cocoa beans to manufacture locally made chocolate, instead of sending its raw produce overseas. The French company Cémoi opened the country's first chocolate factory in May 2015, following President Alassane Ouattara's vision to see the country become a major chocolate manufacturer for the region. Numerous entrepreneurial chocolatiers obliged, opening artisanal chocolate

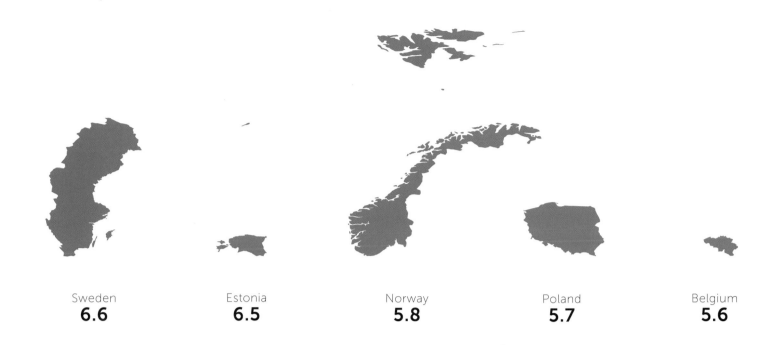

Sweden	Estonia	Norway	Poland	Belgium
6.6	**6.5**	**5.8**	**5.7**	**5.6**

The world's 10 leading chocolate-consuming countries are all in Europe, led by the chocoholics of Switzerland. Figures show per capita consumption, in kilograms.

shops and cafes across Abidjan, in the hope that the country's growing economy will see the average chocolate consumption lift from the current low level of less than 500g (1.1lb) per person per year.

In 2016, the global chocolate industry was worth as much as $98 billion, with the biggest consumers being Germany (7 per cent of global chocolate consumption), the United Kingdom (9 per cent), Russia (11 per cent) and the United States (18 per cent). While every American may have consumed an average of 5.5kg (12lb) of chocolate in 2015, the world's largest per capita consumers of chocolate were, in fact, the Swiss, whose sweet teeth led them to devour an average of 8.8kg (19.4lb) each.

Despite its overwhelming success, this beloved industry is at risk. The likely impacts of climate change in West Africa will include a significant elevating of the optimum growing altitude, right up into the mountains, away from current plantations. Although by no means a death knell for the chocolate industry, this is a reminder of how delicate the whole process is to external pressures. Popular cocoa species have already been decimated by disease, such as the fungus 'witches broom', which wiped out entire plantations in South America during the twentieth century. One of the most commonly grown varieties today is named CCN-51. Far from sweet-sounding, the strain is also widely acknowledged to be less tasty than its predecessors but, with a strong resistance to witches broom, it remains the primary source of cocoa for products demanding bulk orders. So while chocoholics need not worry about losing their favourite treat quite yet, whether future delights will match up to their high standards is a different story.

Flowers

Leading countries by export value of flower bouquets, and the trade flow of the world's largest flower company.

40m   3.5b

US$

Import ——   Export
value   value

Royal FloraHolland

Flowers

The Colombians like to say it with flowers. The country has over 130,000 native plant species, thanks to its warm climate, plentiful rainfall, abundant sunshine and fertile soils. Perhaps this floral diversity was why, in the 1960s, the Alliance for Progress under US President John F. Kennedy recognized Colombia's suitability for industrial flower cultivation. The project, which included a promotional tour to Bogotá in December 1961, was an early USAID (US Agency for International Development) initiative, which sought to use international development as a way to build links between the United States and developing countries. The entrepreneurial American Edgar Wells was one of the first to fully embrace the opportunities this situation presented, setting up an export business that sent Colombian flowers on the new regular flights from Bogota to Miami. His first shipment, $20,000 worth of flowers, was sent in October 1965. 'After 400 years, the true riches of El Dorado have been discovered,' said Wells, 'a permanent source of riches for all Colombians, for all time.'

Wells was somewhat prophetic. Over fifty years later, Colombia's flower exports have blossomed into one of the world's most substantial flower industries, exporting 230,000 tonnes of flowers annually, at a value of $1.3 billion – ahead of Ecuador ($800 million) and Kenya ($675 million) – and growing. This industry is significantly bolstered by the country's strong relationship with the United States, which now imports two-thirds of all cut flowers from Colombia, making the country easily the largest source of flowers in American florists. Colombia has over 4,000 varieties of orchid, more than any other single country, hence why they are one of the most popular farmed flowers, alongside carnations and roses.

Still, even this success is dwarfed by the $3.5 billion's worth of flowers that pass through the Netherlands on an annual basis. As anyone who has cycled the country's famous nationwide bike network will attest, much of rural Netherlands consists of massive, colourful and state-of-the-art greenhouses, cultivating enormous quantities of, predictably, tulips, but also lilies, daffodils and hyacinths. More than 10,000 sq km (4,000 sq miles) of Dutch countryside is currently set aside for outdoor floriculture, equivalent to half the land area of Wales. This includes the vibrant rainbow-coloured fields across the *Bollenstreek* ('bulb region') during the April blooming season.

Despite the number of flower-growing companies in the Netherlands rapidly declining – from 2,269 in 2006 to only 991 in 2016 – the Dutch maintain their place at the top of this most valuable and fragrant industry thanks to the country also acting as a major hub for flowers arriving from outside Europe, such as Colombia.

The small town of Aalsmeer is sometimes known as the flower capital of the world, a reference to the world's largest flower auction that takes place there. Dutch company Royal FloraHolland, based in Aalsmeer, is one of the world's biggest names in the flower trade, exporting more than €6 billion's worth of flowers in 2017, including €785 million to France, €837 million to the United Kingdom and €1.7 billion to Germany. As the Colombians and Dutch are only too aware, there's big business behind that brief romantic gesture.

The symbol of love, the rose, remains the most popular cut flower, a clear winner in Royal FloraHolland's top ten sold cut flowers. Figures show millions of units sold.

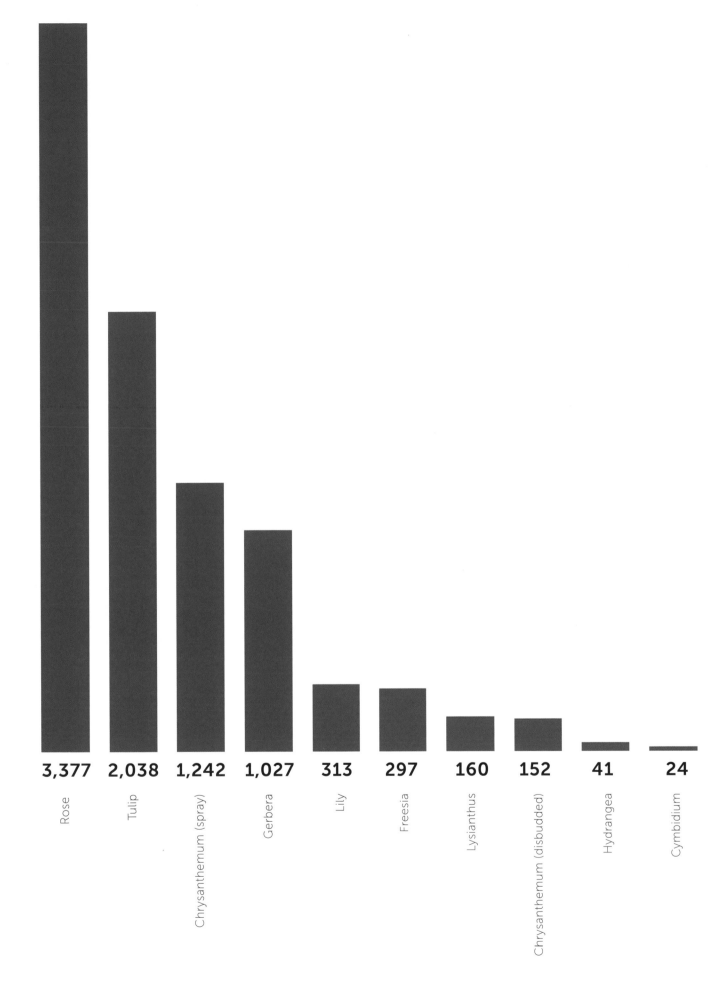

3,377 **2,038** **1,242** **1,027** **313** **297** **160** **152** **41** **24**

Rose

Tulip

Chrysanthemum (spray)

Gerbera

Lily

Freesia

Lysianthus

Chrysanthemum (disbudded)

Hydrangea

Cymbidium

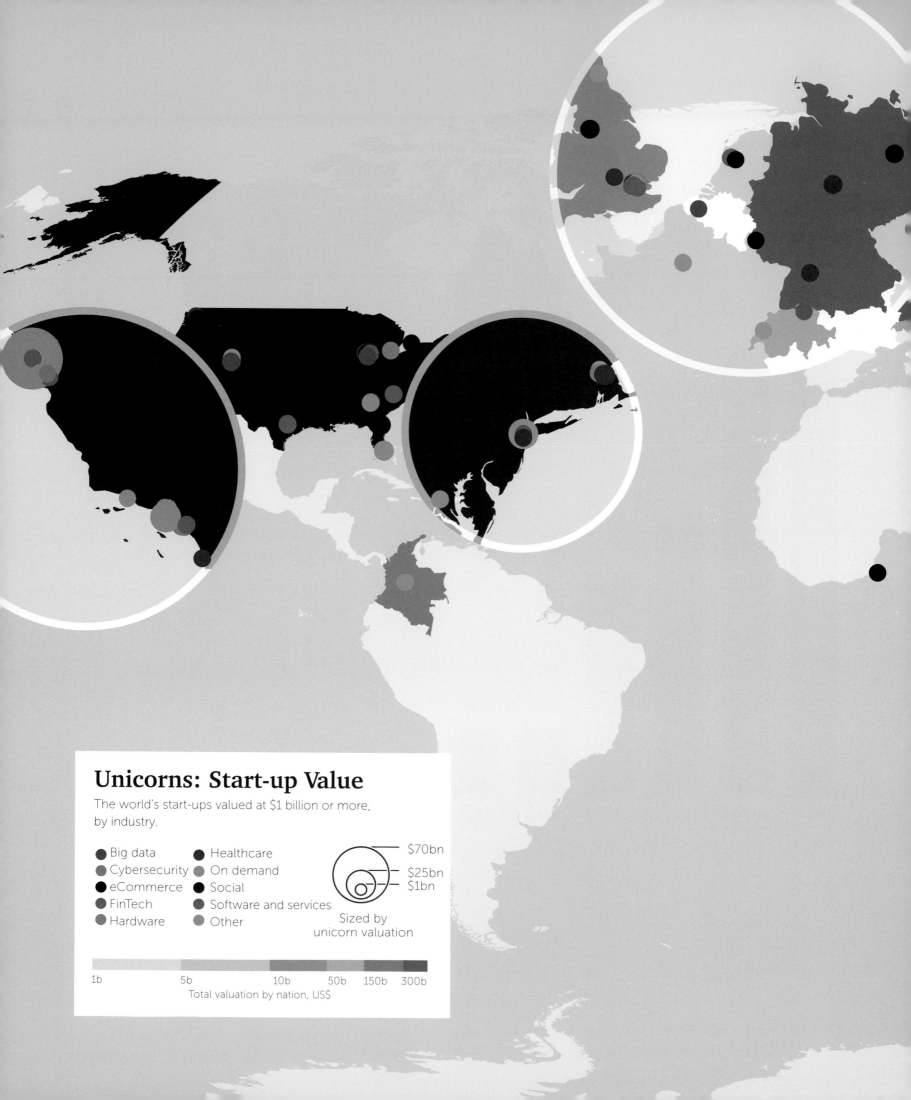

Unicorns: Start-up Value

The world's start-ups valued at $1 billion or more, by industry.

- ● Big data
- ● Cybersecurity
- ● eCommerce
- ● FinTech
- ● Hardware
- ● Healthcare
- ● On demand
- ● Social
- ● Software and services
- ● Other

$70bn
$25bn
$1bn

Sized by unicorn valuation

1b   5b   10b 50b 150b 300b
Total valuation by nation, US$

Unicorns: Funding

Source of funding for the world's start-ups
worth $1b+.

- Big data
- Cybersecurity
- eCommerce
- FinTech
- Hardware
- Healthcare
- On demand
- Social
- Software and services
- Other

Industry

1b   5b   10b   50b   150b   300b

Total valuation by nation, US$

Uber
$68
Airbnb
$29.3

Unicorns

In today's modern, fast-paced economy, there's a certain allure to being the upstart, the innovative, confident new kid on the block, and there are few better ways to achieve this than launching your own business. In recent years entrepreneurs around the world have opted to forego traditional career paths within existing corporations and have, instead, branched out on their own. This has led to an explosion of start-ups, in such diverse fields as hospitality, finance and media, among other industries. Some of these have been so successful that they have been termed 'unicorns', attributable to any startup valued at over $1 billion.

A good example of this is the car-ride-sharing app Uber, which has experienced a phenomenal rise since its conception in 2008. Like so many of its peers, Uber initially started with seed funding – money from early private investors keen to bankroll something they believe will eventually be highly profitable for them – upon launch, at around $200,000. It then began to receive increasingly large sums of money as the company expanded, initially $1.25 million, then $11 million and $32 million, as it moved through various investment rounds. By 2018, these investments totalled over $21 billion. With the company now worth $68 billion, those early Uber investors will have been paid back many times over.

There now exists a rich network of venture capitalist events and partnerships, most famously the US-based seed accelerator Y Combinator, aimed at finding 'the next big thing'. At Y Combinator, aspiring entrepreneurs are invited to pitch their ideas to individuals whose relatively recent successes have healthily bolstered their own bank-account balances by several figures, and who might be able to give start-up wannabes the chance to follow in their footsteps. It is a process that many of the biggest household names in the start-up business have followed.

There's one part of the world that has become synonymous with this kind of get-rich-quick, high-technology venture. Silicon Valley, California, is home

GLOBALOGRAPHY

156

The 5 highest value start-ups, in billion US$. Even some of the world's relatively new companies are now worth multi-billion dollars, with Uber valued at over $68 billion.

Didi Chuxing
$50
Xiaomi
$46
China Internet Plus Holding
(Meituan Dianping)
$30

to everything from major technological corporations such as Apple and Google, as well as 'smaller' companies that include $10 billion cloud-storage website Dropbox and $12.3 billion image-sharing website Pinterest. Even if your start-up isn't located in California, the United States is probably the place to be. For example, the workspace-finding website WeWork is based in New York, the next biggest hub outside of California. Worth more than $20 billion, WeWork provides a platform where employees anywhere in the world can find workspaces no matter which city they physically inhabit.

China's liberal approach to free-spirited, free-market economics has seen the country become the world's other major start-up nation. Particularly successful recent ideas include $46 billion technology company Xiaomi and $56 billion Didi Chuxing, a ride-sharing app like Uber. If the market exists, these start-up networks ensure that any idea can very quickly become worth a billion dollars.

UNICORNS

Airbnb

Number of Airbnb listings in leading cities worldwide.

850   61k

Canada

United States

United Kingdom

Ger

France

Spain

Portugal

Airbnb

In 2007, Brian Chesky and Joe Gebbia posted an advert online, offering air mattresses available for rent for the night on their San Francisco apartment floor. By March 2008, their somewhat quirky idea had caught on – with the somewhat clumsy web address Airbedandbreakfast.com – and had the makings of a successful business. Ten years later, the company had nineteen offices and in excess of a whopping 4.5 million listings worldwide. It also had a snappy new name: Airbnb.

Airbnb allows anyone to post online adverts renting homes out by the bed, by the room, or even to lease out a property in its entirety. For millions of global travellers, Airbnb has become a popular choice among the many websites they can turn to when looking for places to stay in cities around the world. Travellers often save money on what they would otherwise need to pay for a hotel room and, at least according to the promotional material, can enjoy a more 'authentic' experience that allows them to pretend to be actual residents of the city in which they are staying. The top ten countries that visiting guests come from are the United States, France, the United Kingdom, Germany, Australia, Canada, China, Spain, Italy and the Netherlands.

Companies like Airbnb, car-hire firm Uber and numerous others sprung up in the years following the economic crash of 2007–08 with innovative ideas to disrupt traditional industries – such as hotels in Airbnb's case. They use websites and mobile apps as a centralised hub for connecting, for example, people with spare rooms, with people looking for a room for the night. Why exactly Airbnb have so succeeded instead of their many competitors is anyone's guess, but certainly the company has become a figurehead for the new 'sharing economy' that has evolved over the past decade.

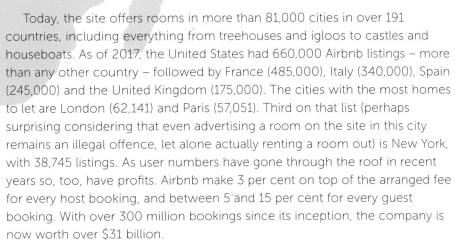

Japan

Australia

Today, the site offers rooms in more than 81,000 cities in over 191 countries, including everything from treehouses and igloos to castles and houseboats. As of 2017, the United States had 660,000 Airbnb listings – more than any other country – followed by France (485,000), Italy (340,000), Spain (245,000) and the United Kingdom (175,000). The cities with the most homes to let are London (62,141) and Paris (57,051). Third on that list (perhaps surprising considering that even advertising a room on the site in this city remains an illegal offence, let alone actually renting a room out) is New York, with 38,745 listings. As user numbers have gone through the roof in recent years so, too, have profits. Airbnb make 3 per cent on top of the arranged fee for every host booking, and between 5 and 15 per cent for every guest booking. With over 300 million bookings since its inception, the company is now worth over $31 billion.

In 2015, Airbnb released details of those neighbourhoods around the world that had the highest growing demand. They included Banglampoo in Bangkok, Thailand; Brickfields in Kuala Lumpur, Malaysia; and Capucins in Bordeaux, France. Top of the list was Chūō-ku in Osaka, Japan, which had grown by 7,000 per cent in just one year. Airbnb noted at the time that all of these neighbourhoods shared certain desirable qualities, such as independent shops, art galleries and recommended food establishments. Tastes of Airbnb customers appear to have matured since a few people were content to pay for an air mattress on the floor for the night.

The 10 leading destinations of inbound Airbnb guests.

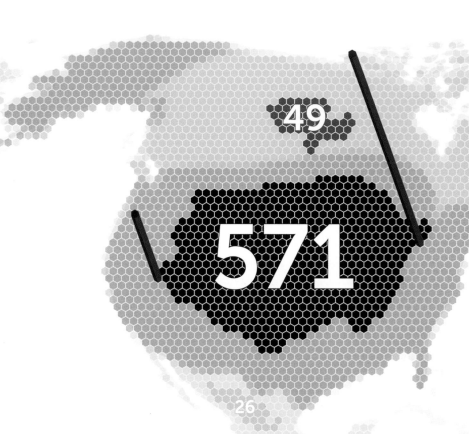

49

571

26

118

51

25

49

Billionaires

The leading 20 countries sized by number of billionaires

Each coloured hexagon represents 1 billionaire

— Fewer   — More   Cities sized by number of billionaires

| 6 | 820 | 4.5k | 19k |

Number of people belonging to the global top 1 per cent of wealth holders, in thousands

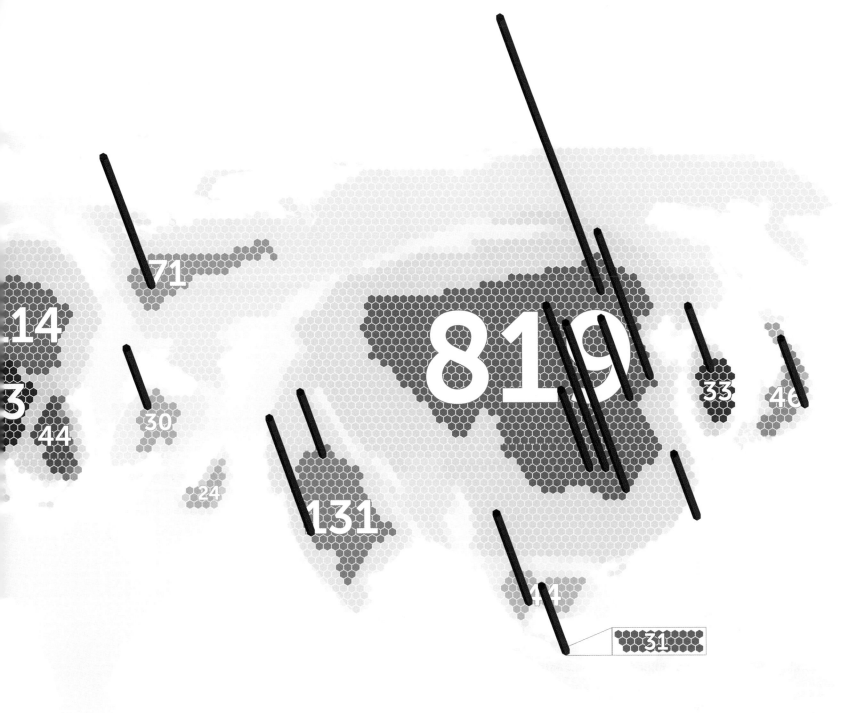

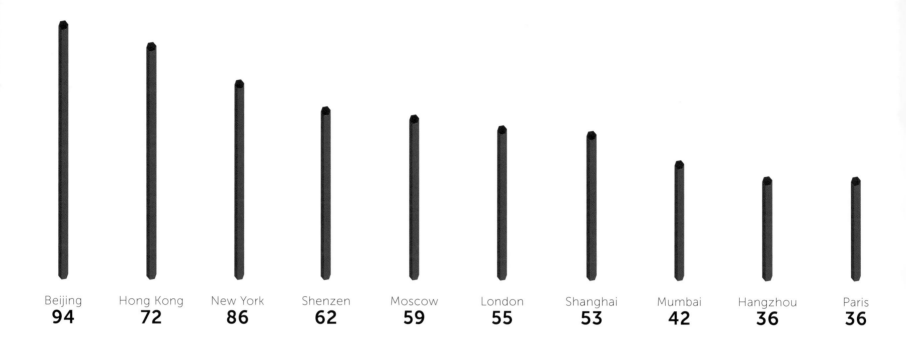

Beijing	Hong Kong	New York	Shenzen	Moscow	London	Shanghai	Mumbai	Hangzhou	Paris
94	**72**	**86**	**62**	**59**	**55**	**53**	**42**	**36**	**36**

Billionaires

With Amazon's Jeff Bezos, Microsoft's Bill Gates and investor Warren Buffett leading the way, it's Americans who sit at the head of the table of the global billionaire's club, with a staggering $3 trillion owned by 571 individuals. Seven of the ten richest people in the world are American – including Facebook's Mark Zuckerberg and Oracle's Larry Ellison - with LVMH's Bernard Arnault from France, Zara CEO Amancio Ortega from Spain and telecommunications tycoon Carlos Slim from Mexico the only non-Americans gatecrashing the top tier. To some, these individuals are inspiring models of the American dream; to others, they are examples of how an intensely capitalist economy can promote a select few individuals to extreme wealth.

Outside of the top ten, Chinese individuals begin to crop up very quickly, primarily in sectors such as real estate and manufacturing, led by WeChat's Ma Huateng and Alibaba's Jack Ma. Between them, China and the United States are now home to half of the more than 2,600 plus billionaires worldwide – a number that is currently increasing year-on-year. It's then a substantial drop down to India, with only 131 billionaires, followed by the United Kingdom (118), Germany (114), Switzerland (83) and Russia (71).

A glance at the cities in which the world's billionaires live reveals how significant a home China has become for the ultra rich, with four of the top five most billionaire-dense cities located in China, namely Beijing (131), Hong Kong (80), Shenzhen (78) and Shanghai (70), with smaller cities such as Hangzhou and Guangzhou rapidly accumulating billionaires. Other major cities near the top of the list include New York (92), London (70) and Moscow (62), an indicator of these and other global cities' ability to concentrate wealth

Seoul	San Francisco	Bangkok	Istanbul	Sao Paolo	Taipei	Singapore	Tokyo	Los Angeles	Guangzhou
30	**29**	**25**	**25**	**25**	**25**	**24**	**24**	**23**	**22**

From highest to lowest, the cities with the most billionaires. Chinese cities are home to the highest numbers of billionaires, and are growing rapidly year-on year.

from around the world. In Asia, these figures also reveal the dominance of major cities in the location of domestic billionaires, with Seoul home to 30 of South Korea's 33 billionaires, and Bangkok home to 43 of the 44 billionaires in Thailand.

Zooming out from a narrow focus on billionaires to look at millionaires reveals the extreme disparity of riches even at the upper end of the wealth pyramid. In China, for example, there were less than two million millionaires in 2017, roughly the same number as Germany, and less than other small countries such as the United Kingdom (2.2 million), Japan (2.7 million) and the US (a whopping 15.4 million). In spite of this, the rapid accumulation of wealth in China due to large-scale manufacturing and booming real estate means that by 2022, the number of Chinese millionaires is expected to grow to 2.7 million people, placing them third on the list behind the US and Japan.

What is truly extraordinary is the extreme concentration of wealth in a handful of individuals in only a select few countries. The world's 36 million millionaires, collectively no more than half a percent of the total adult population, own 46 per cent of total global wealth. In contrast, more than 70 per cent of all adults own less than $10,000 – this is predominantly in the world's developing countries – collectively totalling no more than 3 per cent of global wealth. Crucially, this gap is expanding, with the incomes of the poorest 10 per cent growing by just $65 between 1988 and 2011, while the richest 1 per cent saw their incomes grow by a massive $11,800 during that same time period.

Invasive Species

Overall invasion threat by invasive species.

0.1 0.2 0.3 0.4 0.5 0.6 0.7 0.8 0.9
Threat

No data

Invasive Species

Over a century ago, Fijians were understandably concerned by the impact that rats were having on the local environment. The rodents, introduced by seafaring visitors to the islands, were devouring native bird eggs, seeds and insects. More importantly, as far as the British colonial settlers were concerned, they were proving themselves to be pests in the sugar-cane fields.

The solution, apparently, was to bring in an even more ruthless killer, an expert predator who could control the troublesome rat population: the small Indian mongoose (*Herpestes auropunctatus*). A pair of mongooses were transported from Calcutta to Fiji in 1883, one of many similar Pacific Island introductions. Unfortunately, upon its arrival in Fiji, the mongoose found native wildlife populations that were completely unprepared for such a fast and effective predator. Far from solving the problem, the mongooses exacerbated it. Indigenous birds, reptiles, amphibians and mammals all suffered under the relentless mongoose.

Unfortunately, Fiji was not the only small island on which this live experiment was undertaken. Around the same time, the small Indian mongoose was introduced everywhere from Jamaica to Hawaii, from Mauritius to Barbados. In every case, the predatory mammal proceeded to decimate the local fauna. Furthermore, as a carrier of rabies, it also posed a potential health hazard for humans. While attempts to control the population in the latter half of the twentieth century was successful in eradicating the mongoose from a handful of Fijian islands, its agility and adaptability led, in 2000, to the International Union for Conservation of Nature (IUCN) naming the small Indian mongoose as one of the world's top 100 worst invasive alien species.

The damage caused by the small Indian mongoose in Fiji is just a taste of more recent developments. The IUCN's Red List of Threatened Species shows that invasive species are now the main driver of extinctions worldwide, with everything from rats, goats and pigs to trout, toads and snakes being either accidentally or deliberately introduced into new ecosystems by humans, and then dominating it, wiping native species out.

The level of the threat posed to economies varies dramatically around the world. As some of the most connected countries on Earth, due to their large quantities of agricultural trade, the United States and China are the two biggest sources of invasive species to the rest of the world, followed by other relatively well-connected countries such as Japan, Germany, France and South Korea. Those countries most at risk of being invaded, however, are

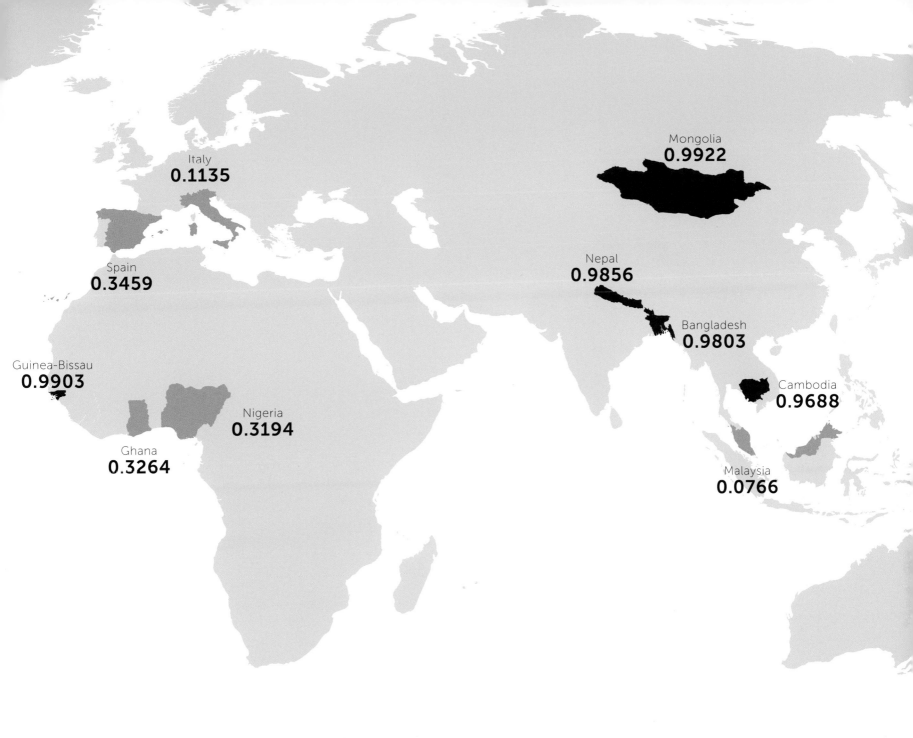

Mongolia
0.9922

Italy
0.1135

Spain
0.3459

Nepal
0.9856

Bangladesh
0.9803

Guinea-Bissau
0.9903

Nigeria
0.3194

Cambodia
0.9688

Ghana
0.3264

Malaysia
0.0766

There is some extreme variation between the 5 most and 5 least at risk countries, based on the overall invasion threat index, calculated from the prospective negative impact on the value of crop exports.

those in the developing world who lack the financial resources and technology to detect and combat a species invasion, such as Guinea-Bissau, Mongolia, Nepal, Bangladesh and Cambodia. The importance of agriculture in these relatively small economies means that they find themselves extremely vulnerable to invasion.

Even neighbours can have strikingly different threat levels from invasive species. For instance, Italy is one of the least at-risk countries, while neighbouring Switzerland is one of the most at-risk countries. Various alien species have found the mountainous Swiss landscape an ideal environment in which to settle and spread, such as the North American racoon, originally introduced to Germany during the 1930s, and Italian crested newts, which escaped from a Geneva research station, and are outcompeting indigenous species. Just as nineteenth-century Fijians found out, native ecosystems can prove surprisingly fragile when invasive species get out of hand.

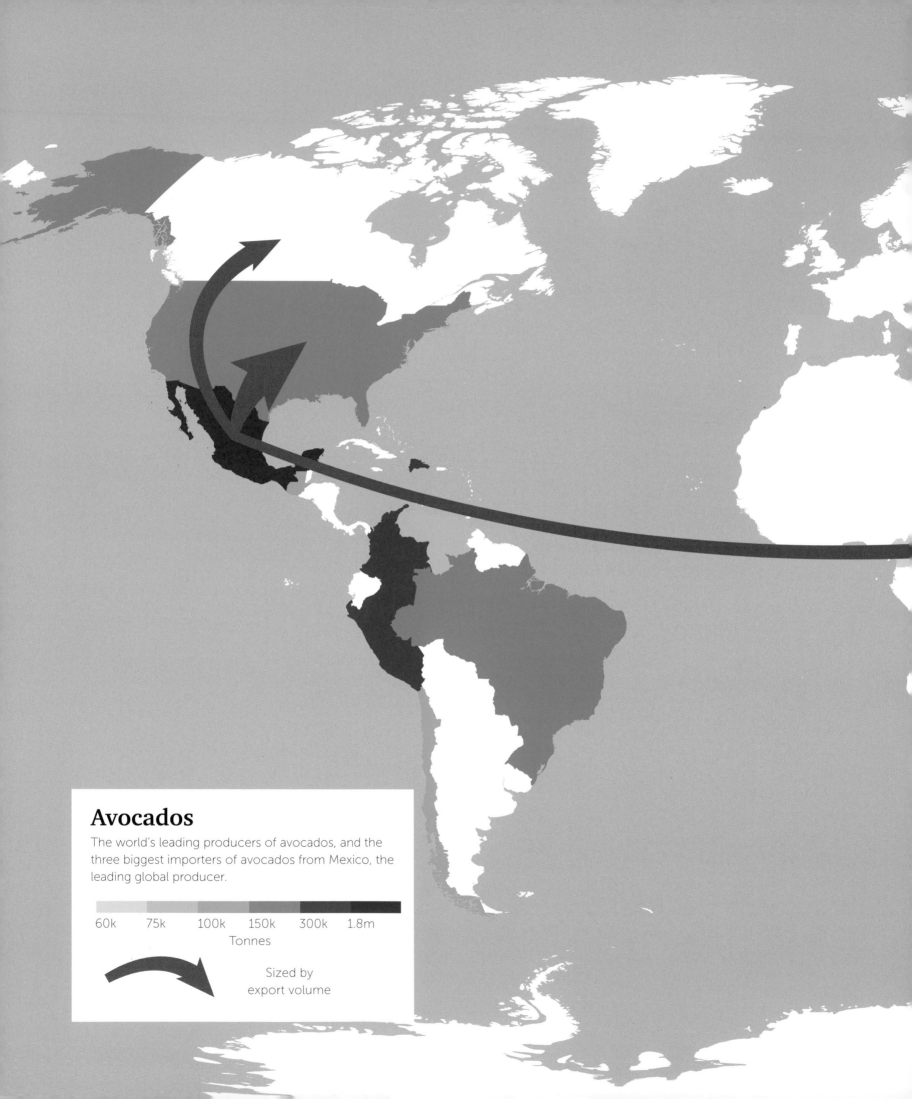

Avocados

The world's leading producers of avocados, and the three biggest importers of avocados from Mexico, the leading global producer.

60k   75k   100k   150k   300k   1.8m
Tonnes

Sized by
export volume

Avocados

Global consumption of the avocado, and the humble Hass in particular, has escalated dramatically since the turn of the millennium – in part, the result of growing trends for healthy eating, but also thanks to the fruit having become more widely available. There is also something to be said for producers managing to guarantee ripe-and-ready-to-eat avocados on arrival at their end destination.

This combination of factors has had considerable impact. Whereas a total of 2.7 million tonnes of the creamy fruit was produced in 2000, by 2016, the figure had more than doubled to 5.6 million tonnes.

Front and centre of the avocado boom is the country that can claim to be the fruit's spiritual home: Mexico. Spanish conquistadors encountered the avocado when they arrived during the sixteenth century, and there is evidence aplenty that it has been cultivated in Mexico for as many as 9,000 years. Along the so-called 'avocado belt', which stretches across the centre of the country through the states of Mexico and Michoacán, business is booming, trees are felled and there is fierce rivalry over the opportunity to plant and profit from the increased popularity of the avocado. Mexico alone produced nearly 1.9 million tonnes of avocados in 2016, more than three times that of the next highest producer, the Dominican Republic (600,000 tonnes). Other significant producers were Peru (455,000 tonnes), Colombia (309,000 tonnes) and Indonesia (305,000 tonnes).

While the demand for avocados has clearly risen globally, there can be few more dramatic dietary shifts than that seen in the United States, where average avocado consumption has escalated from 1kg (2.2lb) in 2000, to 3.2kg (7.1lb) by 2016. Indeed, the United States is the number one destination for Mexico's million of tonnes of avocados, with more than three-quarters of the country's 870,000 tonnes exported in 2016 crossing the border to the north, a trend that has been gradually building ever since the North American Free Trade Agreement of 1994 enabled Mexican growers to sell their produce into the North American market tariff-free.

Of Mexico's remaining avocado exports, 71,000 tonnes went ever further north, to Canada, 61,000 tonnes travelled all the way across the Pacific Ocean to Japan, and the rest were scattered around the world. China has also become a booming market for avocados in recent years, with imports from Mexico leaping from just 470 tonnes in 2013, to 11,000 tonnes three years later. South Korea's recent infatuation with the avocado has been even more dramatic, with imports leaping from $750,000 worth of avocados in

United States
668K

Japan
62K

Canada
72K

The three largest importers of Mexican avocados, in tonnes. The popularity of guacamole is one reason why the US is easily the world's biggest importer of avocados.

September 2016, to $2.4 million just twelve months later. The rising popularity of such trendy foods as avocado toast in Asia means demand for avocados in the region is set to rise higher and higher.

Rich in fats, vitamins and minerals, the avocado's health benefits are undeniable. It is also highly versatile and easy to prepare, making it a ready staple in salads, sandwiches and dips. When quizzed over their increased interest in avocados, more than three-quarters of North Americans favoured the nutritional benefits of the fruit, while a similar number expressed a fondness for the taste. Certainly, such huge newfound popularity of the fruit suggests that this is not just a fad among the young and trendy, but a lasting addition to the North American diet.

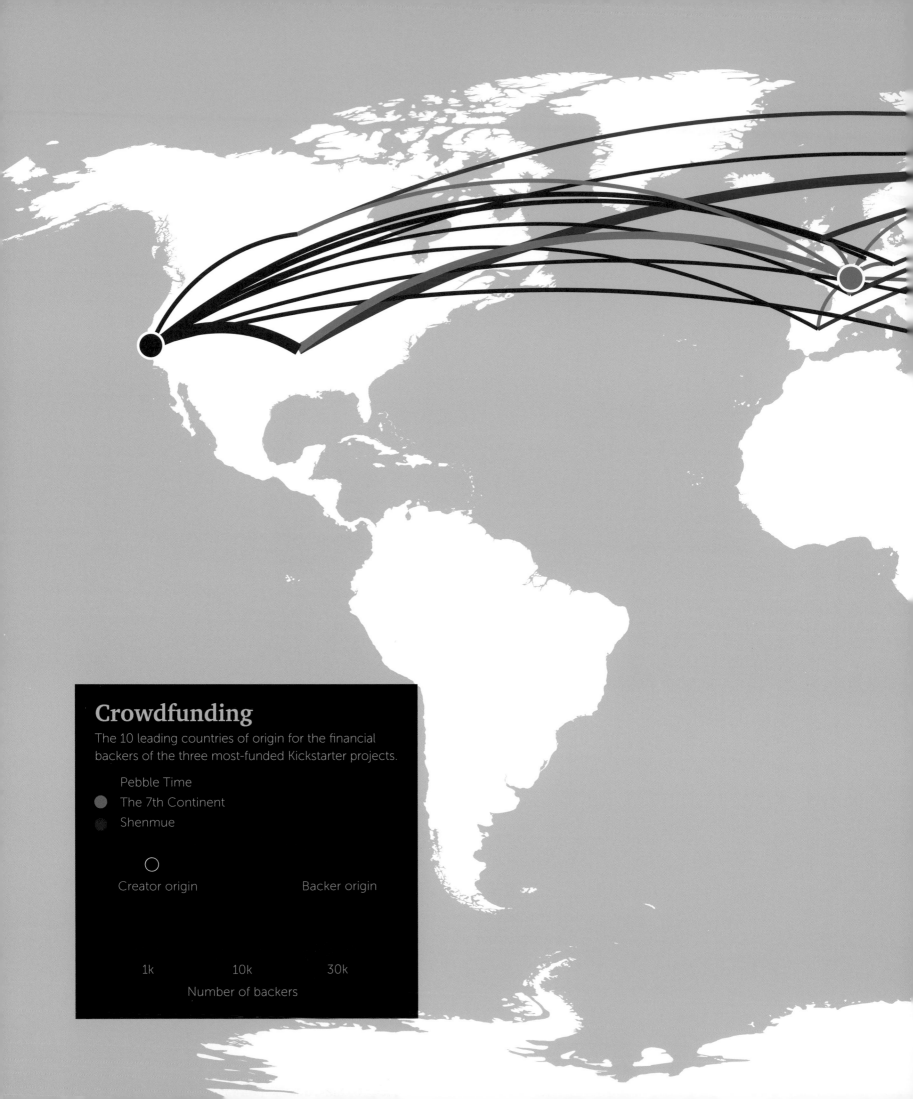

Crowdfunding

The 10 leading countries of origin for the financial
backers of the three most-funded Kickstarter projects.

- Pebble Time
- The 7th Continent
- Shenmue

○ Creator origin   Backer origin

1k   10k   30k
Number of backers

Seattle
554

Toronto
791

London
2,354

San Francisco
984

New York
887

Los Angeles
756

Crowdfunding

The Pebble is a wristwatch that has the honourable distinction of being the world's first commercial smartwatch, the precursor to contemporary products such as the Apple Watch and Fitbit. Utilizing innovative 'e-paper' technology as a screen display, the Pebble came to international attention in May 2012 because of the unique way in which it was funded to the tune of more than $10 million. The money wasn't invested by one company, nor was it money borrowed from a bank. Instead, every penny spent on the research, development and execution of turning the idea of the Pebble into a reality was through donations that came via the internet, from future customers putting their money where their respective mouths were and pledging to pay for their Pebble in advance. It is a story that has been replayed over and over again in the revolutionary world of crowdfunding.

In principle, crowdfunding refers to nothing more than a large group of people each pledging to pay what they feel is a reasonable amount of money in order to get an idea – whether it be a product, like the Pebble, a creative project, or maybe a charitable endeavour – off the ground. The thing that has given the concept a major boost in recent years is the internet, which has seen the rise of reputable, big-name middleman websites, such as Kickstarter—which Pebble used for its fundraising. Around one-third of the 400,000 projects launched on Kickstarter by early 2018 have been successful, primarily focused on music and film projects and, to a lesser extent, on games, publishing, art and design projects (technology projects, such as the Pebble, have actually been a fairly niche category, although often the most expensive).

As the home of major crowdfunding websites Kickstarter, GoFundMe and Indiegogo, the United States dominates the majority of projects available for funding, claiming half of nearly 8,000 currently active projects globally. The United Kingdom is the only country that comes close to competing with this,

Led by London and Singapore, the top cities backing Pebble Time – the most-funded Kickstarter campaign – by number of backers.

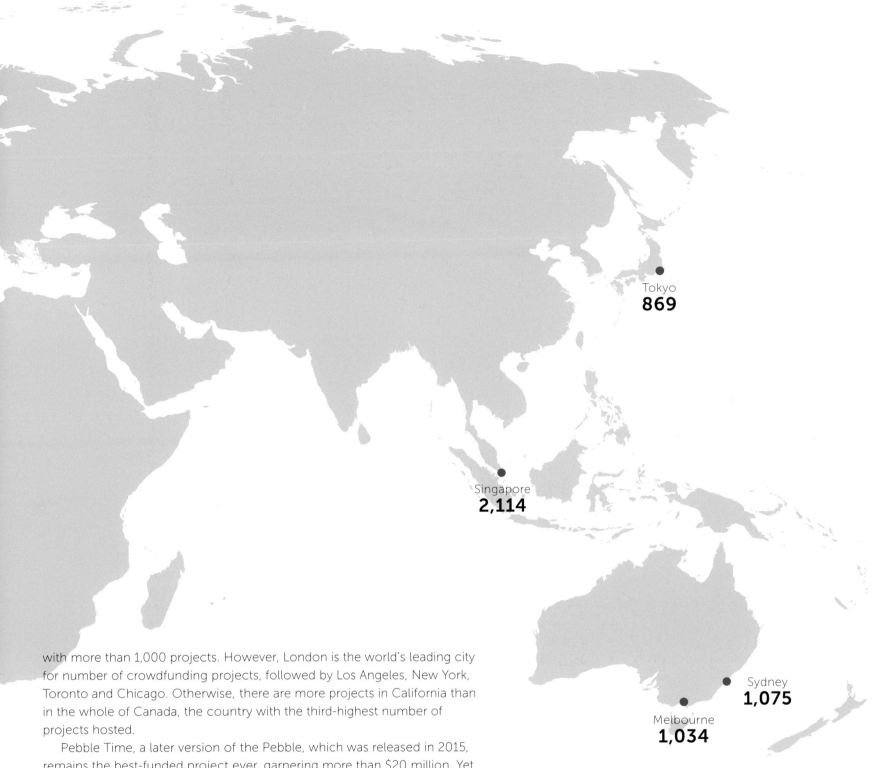

Tokyo
869

Singapore
2,114

Sydney
1,075

Melbourne
1,034

with more than 1,000 projects. However, London is the world's leading city for number of crowdfunding projects, followed by Los Angeles, New York, Toronto and Chicago. Otherwise, there are more projects in California than in the whole of Canada, the country with the third-highest number of projects hosted.

Pebble Time, a later version of the Pebble, which was released in 2015, remains the best-funded project ever, garnering more than $20 million. Yet time has not been kind to the Pebble Technology Corporation. With finances increasingly tight, and sales limited to just 100,000 over three months, the company's intellectual property was bought by rival Fitbit in December 2016, and its groundbreaking products discontinued. Yet while the Pebble has suffered in the long term, the amount of money raised through Kickstarter, and other crowdfunding sites, continues to escalate rapidly. In 2012, when the Pebble was making waves around the world, a total of $275 million had been pledged to Kickstarter projects. This hit $1 billion by early 2014, $2 billion by late 2015, and by early 2018 there had been over $3.5 billion pledged to all Kickstarter projects. Keen to launch the next big thing? Simply ask people to pledge for it.

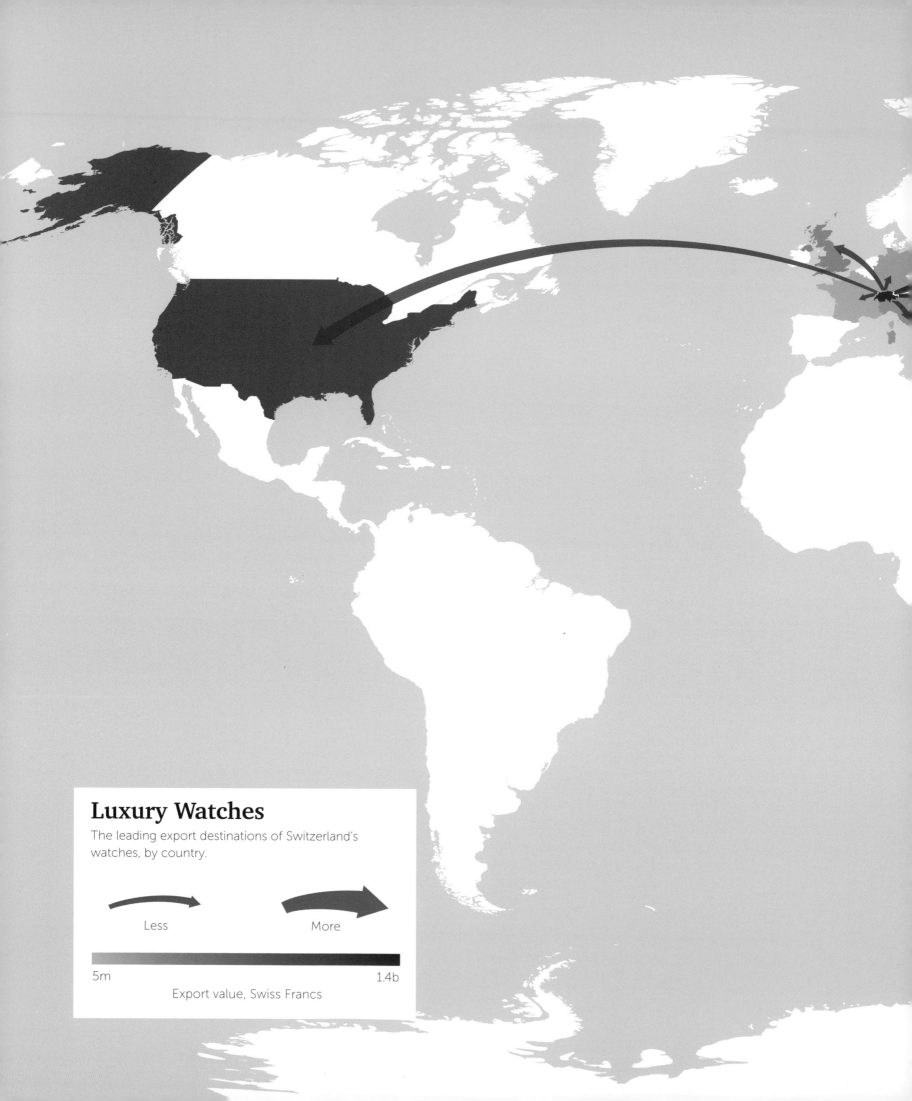

Luxury Watches

The leading export destinations of Switzerland's watches, by country.

Less   More

5m   1.4b

Export value, Swiss Francs

Luxury Watches

Wearing your status on your sleeve dates back to the dawn of watchmaking. With luxury watches by brands such as Rolex selling for many thousands of dollars, their popularity among the rich and famous relates to more than simply being able to tell the time accurately. A luxury watch advertises the identity of its wearer, their personality, their aspirations. And there can surely be few countries so proud of their manufacturing of one product as the Swiss are of their luxury watches. The luxury-watch industry contributes around 10 per cent of Swiss national exports, employing up to 57,000 people across 700 companies. At over $8 billion, Swiss luxury manufacturer Rolex was the world's fifth most valuable luxury brand in 2017, behind fashion brands Chanel, Gucci, Hermes and Louis Vuitton.

These days, 'Swiss-made' is a much harder term to define than might initially be imagined. Until recently, gaining such an official label meant that at least 50 per cent of a watch was built inside the Alpine nation, a figure raised to 60 per cent in 2017 in response to various manufacturers trying to cut costs by having as many components of their products manufactured overseas as the rules would allow. Despite national pride at the thought of manufacturing the world's highest-quality timepieces entirely by themselves, the global economy instead sees the Swiss dependent on numerous countries for everything from parts (such as straps from Italy and France, and cases from China and Hong Kong) to even manufacturing (increasingly taking place in Thailand and Mauritius).

Nevertheless, the difficulties of the modern watch industry are nothing compared to the great 'watch crisis' of the 1970s and 1980s. Following the arrival of the Japanese Seiko Astron 35SQ, wrists around the world started switching from the expensive mechanical watches that the Swiss specialised in, to relatively cheap watches controlled instead by quartz. The Swiss found their effective monopoly over the world's watch supply rapidly diminishing. It was only the creation of the quartz Swatch ('second watch') in 1982 that eventually began the great revival, quickly growing to sell more than one million units in the first year. Despite being branded as a cheap, mass-produced commodity, rare, limited-edition of Swatches released over the subsequent years have on occasion sold for up to $20,000, more than even the luxury Rolexes and Omegas at the top end of the market.

In 2016, Switzerland was easily the largest exporter of watches by value, $19.1 billion – primarily mechanical watches – to major export destinations including Hong Kong, the United States, mainland China, Italy, Japan and

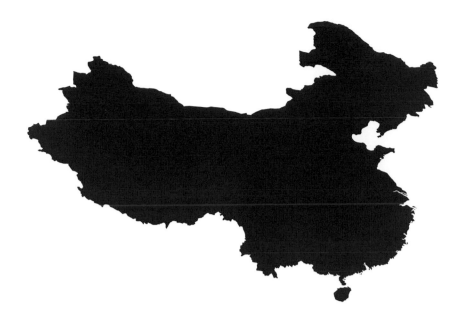

China
893 million units, $14.4 billion export value

Switzerland
25.4 million units, $19.1 billion export value

Switzerland may export only a fraction of the number of watches as China, but their luxury status means they still make more money.

Germany, all countries with significant numbers of people eager for a status symbol to show off their financial success. Significantly, these sales came from only 25.4 million units, whereas China, the next highest exporter of watches, made only $5.6 billion from an incredible 652 million watches (plus $8.8 billion taken from 241 million units through Hong Kong specifically). Ranging in price from under $200 to more than $3,000, the average export price of a Swiss watch is $708 (significantly more than the average of $4 taken from exported Chinese watches). These figures firmly underline the two extremes of the market in which these two countries are operating. Regardless of what future challenges lie ahead, Swiss watch aficionados can enjoy paying the uniquely high prices they appear to still be willing to pay out for a watch bearing the stamp 'Swiss-made'.

Paper Packaging

Leading countries sized by total pulp usage for production of wrapping and packaging paper.

38.0k   66.5m

Pulp, tonnes

100m

50m

100k

Paper and paperboard production, tonnes

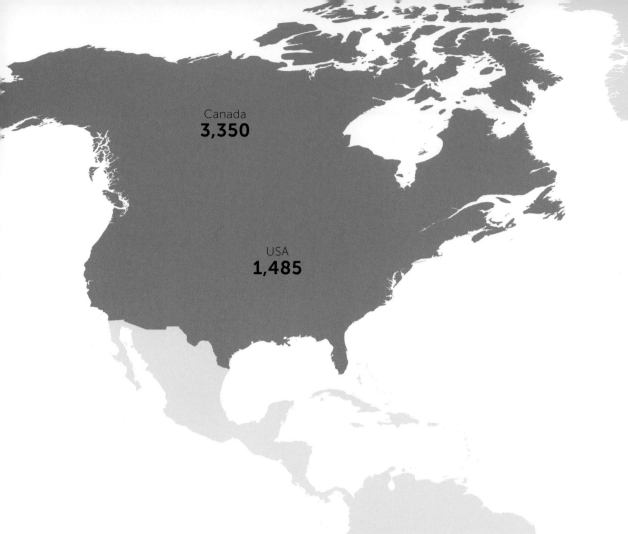

Canada
3,350

USA
1,485

Paper Packaging

For Finland, trees are everything. Three-quarters of the country's total land area is forested with species such as pine, spruce and birch. For centuries, Finland's forests have been the source of multiple domestic industries shipping such products as timber and tar across borders as part of an early trading network. Despite a turndown that has seen a slump in forest-related products in recent decades, 43,000 Finns continue to work in the country's forest industry – known as *metsäteollisuus*.

At the forefront of this, the paper industry has been a cornerstone of the Finnish economy ever since the first manually powered paper mill was established in 1667. Some 350 years later, the industry turns over €19 billion every year, and Finland is home to UPM-Kymmene, one of the biggest names in global paper. Finland now produces over 10 million tonnes of paper and pulp (the moist, fibrous raw material which is turned into paper) every year, and with a population of only 5.5 million people, and therefore a domestic annual consumption of only 1.1 million tonnes, it enables more than 90 per cent of that to be exported. By comparison, local demands mean that just over 5 per cent of the 110 million tonnes of pulp China produces on an annual basis is exported, with the rest going into paper and cardboard manufacturing.

More than 400 million tonnes of paper and cardboard are produced from pulp globally every year, with the world's highest production taking pace in

Germany
1,906

Japan
2,906

China
2,600

China, the United States, Japan and Germany. In each country, the huge domestic paper production feeds domestic demands almost entirely, leaving very little leftover for export, hence most of these top paper producers keep their manufactured products within their own borders.

However, demands for paper and pulp vary dramatically by country. For example, Germany and the United States are both major exporters of pulp and paper, yet both are also major importers from other countries with speciality paper production. For example, Canada is the world's leading producer of newsprint. Led by companies such as Resolute Forest Products in Montreal they turned pulp into 3.35 million tonnes of newsprint in 2016. While Canada certainly has a healthy newspaper industry, it is not so healthy that it creates enough newspapers to use that much newsprint. Instead, significant quantities of it are exported around the world. Other countries, such as Brazil, Mexico and Italy, use pulp in the production of sanitary paper (such as tissues and paper towels), respectively 1.15 million, 1.19 million and 1.48 million tonnes in 2016. The United States and China are, however, the world's largest producers in the manufacturing of wrapping and packaging paper. Their 46.45 million tonnes and 66.55 million tonnes, respectively, dwarf volumes from other countries, numbers that even the Finns cannot complete with.

The 5 leading producing countries of pulp for newsprint, in thousand tonnes.

Canada

United States

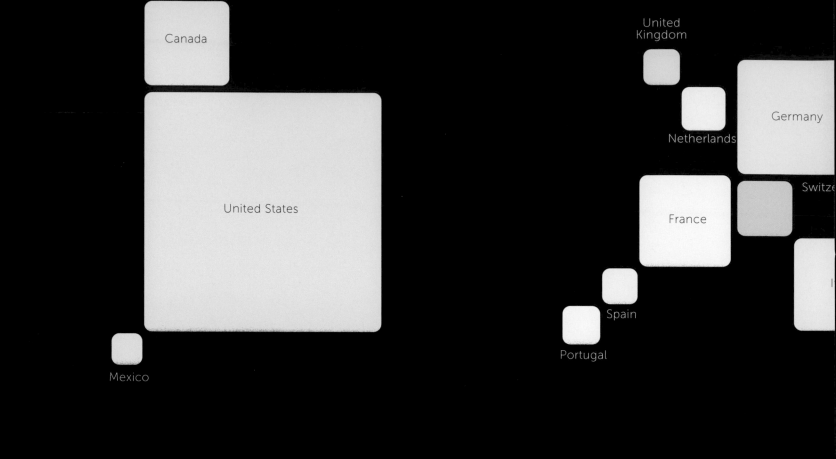

United
Kingdom

Netherlands

Germany

Switze

France

Spain

Portugal

Mexico

Peru

Brazil

Chile

European
Central Bank

Gold

Leading countries based on gold export value, and
gold reserves of the largest gold holding countries
worldwide.

10   82.3
Export value, million US$

Less
More

Reserve size

International
Monetary Fund

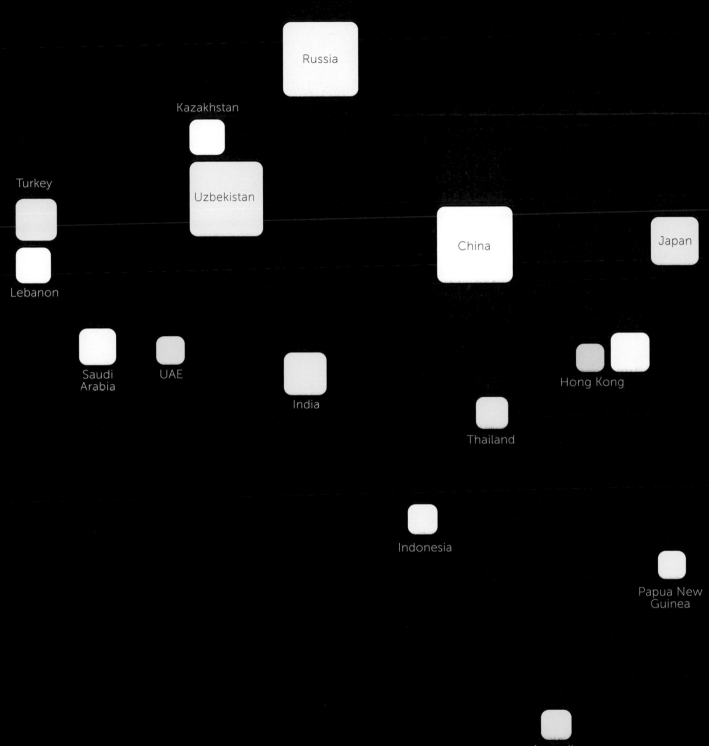

Russia

Kazakhstan

Turkey

Uzbekistan

Lebanon

China

Japan

Saudi
Arabia

UAE

India

Hong Kong

Thailand

Indonesia

Papua New
Guinea

Australia

outh Africa

Canada
180

United States
245

Gold

As good as gold. Having a heart of gold. Worth its weight in gold. As the lexicon of at least the English language testifies, society places a great value on this particular malleable precious metal. Even other materials are compared to it; crude oil is nicknamed 'liquid gold', coal is 'black gold' and saffron was once so valuable it was known as 'red gold'. For centuries, ships have been launched and wars waged by people desperate to get their hands on all kinds of golden treasures.

In the twenty-first century, gold remains as valuable as ever, commanding as much as $1,250 per troy ounce in 2016. Only fifteen years earlier, the price of gold was a mere $270 per troy ounce, while in 2012 it had soared to $1,650 – evidence that the price has fluctuated hugely since the turn of the new millennium. One explanation for this comes from the exponential rise in technology in modern life; tiny fragments of gold can be found in everything from circuit boards to space telescopes. The application of gold in nanotechnology may see gold used in such innovations as solar panelling and smart clothes in the near future.

Still, at least half of the current demand for gold derives from its use in jewellery. In China, the world's largest consumer of gold, more than half of imported gold is used for the manufacture of jewellery, far ahead of the amount turned into gold bars, gold coins or for industrial purposes. Patently, the most popular use for this particular commodity is to wear it on your person, adding a degree of ambiguity as to the exact quantifiable value, which is something few other metals have to contend with.

With such high value placed upon this iconic dusty-yellow metal, it should come as no surprise to learn that there is much interest in knowing who owns the most gold in the world. Many of the wealthiest countries hold large

Russia
255

China
440

Australia
300

volumes of the precious metal, locked away in vaults, among them France and Italy (2,450 tonnes each) and Germany (3,400 tonnes). However, with more than 8,100 tonnes, the world's biggest national hoard belongs to the United States – much of it kept in the compound in Kentucky known as Fort Knox, made famous by the 1964 James Bond movie *Goldfinger*. Today, Fort Knox houses as much as 4.2 million kg (147.3 million oz) of gold, stored in 11.3-kg (400-oz) bars, and worth a reported $200 billion. Another country famous for keeping large volumes of wealth under lock and key is Switzerland, currently the world's largest exporter of gold, selling over $82 billion in 2016, far ahead of the $54 billion exported from Hong Kong, or the relatively smaller amounts exported from the United Arab Emirates, the US or the United Kingdom.

Despite these impressive numbers, considerably more gold remains below ground than has ever been mined to the surface. Compared to the 3,000 tonnes mined in 2015, and the 34,000 tonnes kept in central banks and private funds worldwide, there is an estimated 56,000 tonnes still stored underground in mine reserves. Russia and South Africa have some of the largest mine reserves in the world, with around 5,500 and 6,000 tonnes respectively, while the country sitting on by far the largest reserves in the world is Australia, with an estimated 9,800 tonnes. The opportunity to make your fortune by digging for gold drove many emigrants to Australia, especially Western Australia, during the late nineteenth and early twentieth centuries. More than one hundred years on, the taste for this precious metal appears to have returned with a vengeance.

GOLD

The 5 leading countries in mine production of gold worldwide, in tonnes.

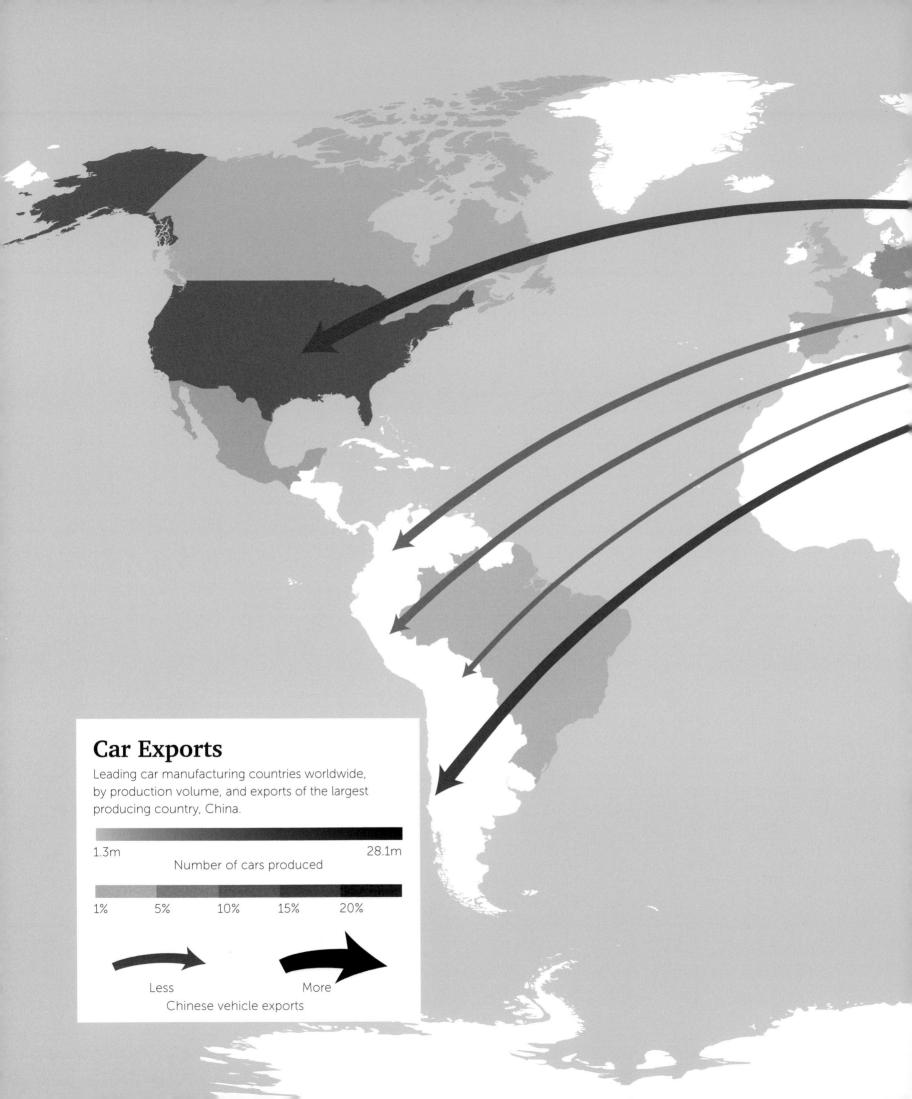

Car Exports

Leading car manufacturing countries worldwide, by production volume, and exports of the largest producing country, China.

1.3m   28.1m

Number of cars produced

1%   5%   10%   15%   20%

Less   More

Chinese vehicle exports

Car Exports

In 1886, the German engineer Karl Benz was awarded a patent for his invention, a horseless three-wheel carriage created by inserting an internal combustion engine into what is now recognized as the very first motorcar. Twenty years later, American business magnate Henry Ford developed the Model T, the mass production of which made the vehicle relatively inexpensive compared to those of rival manufacturers, kickstarting an industry that went on to define much of the modern world.

In 2017, nearly 26 million commercial vehicles and more than 79 million passenger cars were produced globally – figures that are estimated to rise to a combined 107 million by 2020. Germany, Japan and the United States, each critical to the development of the car through the twentieth century, are still core global production markets today. Big-name manufacturers including Volkswagen, Toyota and Ford remain among the world's biggest automobile brand names. However, none of these countries match China when it comes to being the world's largest single manufacturer of modern cars.

In 2017, China saw nearly 25 million cars roll off the production line – more than three times the number produced in Japan, the world's second-largest manufacturer. Significantly, the country has few strong automobile brand names of its own, instead embracing joint global ventures between domestic manufacturers and leading, trusted global brands from overseas – Shanghai General Motors Company and Shanghai Volkswagen Automotive Company, for example – to produce a vast number of cars, the majority of which remain within China. The rise in domestic demand is staggering, with sales in passenger cars shooting from 4 million in 2005, to 21 million by 2015.

The 6 leading markets for plug-in electric passenger car sales, as a percentage of total passenger car sales. When it comes to the next generation of plug-in electric cars, Norwegians are the highest consumers.

Those that are exported find their way as far afield as Egypt, Vietnam, Chile and India, where Western-made cars are prohibitively expensive. The most popular single destination for cars exported from China is Iran, which accounts for as much as 20 per cent of all Chinese-made cars. Economic and trade sanctions made in 2012 forbade companies from many countries operating within Iran, and European corporations such as Renault and Peugeot were forced out of the country. This made way for lesser-known Chinese brands such as Chery, Lifan and Changan to fulfil Iranian demand. Today, the China–Iran path is a substantial one in global car trade.

Chinese car manufacturers such as Geely are now set to take on Germany and the United States as some of the most famous carmakers in the world. Nevertheless, in the long term, the future is uncertain for traditional car sales. While demand is expected to keep growing well into the 2020s, the rise of both electric and driverless cars is introducing unpredictability into the industry. From only 100,000 back in 2012, there were around 1.2 million active electric vehicles in use worldwide in 2016. Manufactured primarily in Germany, the United States and China, the electric car currently enjoys by far the greatest number of sales in China, while Norway has the largest proportion of electric cars compared to the rest of the vehicles on the roads – driven by government policies to phase out petrol and diesel cars by 2025 – followed by the Netherlands and Sweden. Similarly, the global market for autonomous driving hardware is anticipated to grow from $400 million in 2015 to $40 billion by 2030. The humble car may be set for as much innovation in the next few years as it saw in the early days of Benz and Ford.

Honey

Leading countries by export quantity of natural honey, and number of beehives in leading countries.

41.5   276.6

Tonnes

100   1k   10k   100k   1m   10m   12m

Beehives

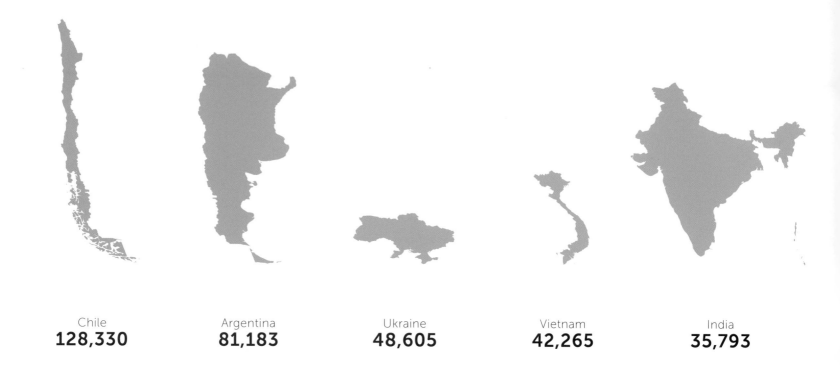

Chile	Argentina	Ukraine	Vietnam	India
128,330	**81,183**	**48,605**	**42,265**	**35,793**

Honey

The *Ramayana* is an ancient Sanskrit epic told over seven books, a fictional tale following the protagonist Prince Rama's quest to recover his wife Sita, a narrative that has since been reinvented within India to refer, in general, to the triumph of good over evil. In the story, we meet King Sugriva, ruler of the monkey kingdom, who maintains the region of Madhuban (meaning 'forest of honey') for the keeping of bees, from whom honey was extracted using the crude method of simply squeezing it out from the hive. Dating back over two thousand years, this is one of the very earliest references to Indian beekeeping. Today, the humble bee provides millions of Indians with their livelihoods, as the country churns out tens of thousands of bee-related products.

Despite their rich heritage, organized commercial beekeeping didn't take off in India until the late nineteenth century, when modern hives were introduced to the country. Post-independence, beekeeping was extensively promoted by the government as a way of economically invigorating rural parts of the country. Thanks primarily to the vast scale of the country, beekeeping in India has since grown and grown; in 2016 the country claimed nearly 12.5 million beehives, considerably more than China, Turkey, Iran or Ethiopia, the other most beehive-populated countries in the world. Globally, the agricultural harvesting of bees has gradually grown in popularity, with the world's total number of beehives climbing from nearly 80 million in 2010, to over 90 million by 2016.

It isn't just honey that keeps beekeepers in business, as is evident from the dominant commodity derived in the top two beehive countries. India focuses

Mexico	Spain	Brazil	Germany	Belgium
29,098	**27,422**	**24,203**	**23,795**	**20,816**

on beeswax, with as much as 23,500 tonnes produced domestically in 2016 (for comparison, the next highest was Ethiopia, with only 5,500 tonnes). This raw material – a by-product of traditional honey production, obtainable when beekeepers crack open honeycombs – is very important in the creation of candles, especially for use in religious ceremonies, but it can also be used for everything from furniture and floor waxes to waxed paper and cosmetics. China, on the other hand, is the world's biggest producer of natural honey, a massive 491,000 tonnes (the second largest, Turkey, managed a mere 106,000). What the Chinese don't consume, they export, with around one-third of Chinese honey shipped abroad, at a value of nearly $300 million. The largest demand for both these products comes from the United States, which imported 3,462 tonnes of beeswax and nearly 153,000 tonnes of natural honey (Germany imported 3,337 tonnes of beeswax and 88,000 tonnes of natural honey, the second highest in both categories).

Especially in Europe (but also in North America) honeybees have become increasingly threatened by colony collapse disorder over the past decade, a phenomenon that results in the sudden and seemingly unexplained deaths of an entire colony of bees. Possible causes include everything from the rampant overuse of pesticides in agriculture, to stress caused by a lack of viable food sources, resulting in poor nutrition and immune systems. Either way, it has increased demand on overseas sources of honey and beeswax for European customers, presumably making them all the more grateful to overseas beekeepers.

Export value of the leading natural honey exporters worldwide, by country, in million US$.

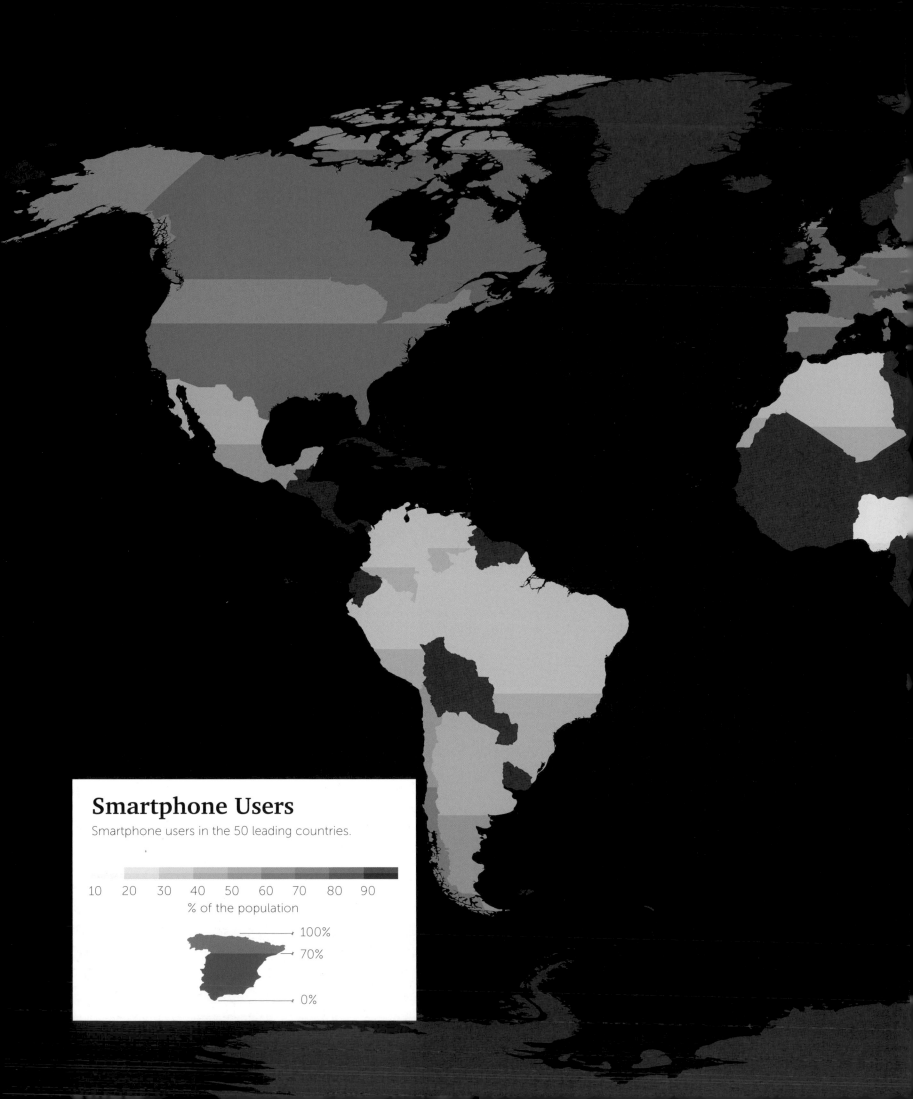

Smartphone Users

Smartphone users in the 50 leading countries.

10 20 30 40 50 60 70 80 90

% of the population

100%
70%
0%

Smartphone Users

Attendees of the 1992 COMDEX conference in Las Vegas, Nevada – a now-defunct computer expo trade show – were lucky enough to witness what could well be described as a moment in history. Among all the other technological marvels displayed at this particular event, it is the IBM/BellSouth product that has stood the test of time. Capable of making phone calls, performing calculations and storing addresses, as well as sending and receiving emails, documents and even faxes, their latest device, the Simon Personal Communicator – codenamed 'Angler' – was the first portable phone to have a touchscreen enabling multiple capabilities beyond those of your basic telephone. In other words, it was the world's very first smartphone.

Unfortunately for the Simon Personal Communicator, several factors limited its commercial success. By the time the device finally hit stores, in August 1994 – almost two years after its unveiling – it weighed in at 0.5kg (1 lb), was 3.8cm (1.5in) thick and cost a pricey $1,100. It had no web browser (not that there were many websites to browse back then) and, of course, no app store. Ultimately, the product was on sale for no more than two years, shifting around 50,000 units, before eventually being discontinued. The phone's greatest failure, according to the experts, was its distressingly short battery life.

Somewhat staggeringly to think of now, back in 1994 there were only 56 million mobile subscribers in the entire world. In 2007, however, with a total of 3.4 billion mobile subscribers populating the planet, Apple's Steve Jobs stood on a platform and famously announced the release of the very first iPhone. Weighing just 135g (4.75oz) and costing between $500 and $600, it went on to achieve what the Simon Personal Communicator never could, and made smartphone capabilities mainstream. Within a year the first Android smartphone was released, and the next stage of competition was underway.

By 2016 there were more than 7.7 billion mobile subscribers in the world (a number that is greater than the world's population), an estimated 2.1 billion of which were smartphone users. Quarter by quarter, South Korea's Samsung jostles with Apple in the United States for the title of the world's largest smartphone manufacturer, each shipping around 75 million units per quarter (both far ahead of other rivals such as LG, Huawei and Alcatel). China's

2017	**1,536.54**
2016	**1,495.96**
2015	**1,423.9**
2014	**1,244.74**
2013	**969.72**
2012	**680.11**
2011	**472**
2010	**296.65**
2009	**172.38**
2008	**139.29**
2007	**122.32**

The number of smartphones sold to end users worldwide from 2007 to 2017, in million units. In just a decade, smartphones have gone from being a niche luxury product, to a ubiquitous device found in the pockets of billions of people.

smartphone usage, in particular, is rapidly escalating, almost doubling from 436 million users in 2013 to an anticipated 817 million by 2022.

Across every continent, mobile devices are shipped in huge numbers, with apps utilizing communication technologies such as GPS (global positioning system) and VoIP (voice over internet protocol) to fulfil the world's desire to chat, tap and surf to its heart's content. The era for the Simon Personal Communicator has finally arrived, if only the device itself hadn't been so far ahead of its time.

Cotton

The world's leading producers, importers and exporters of cotton. Countries sized by cotton production.

1.0k   7.4m

Number of bales (480lb) imported

14.8m
500k
1k

Sized by number of bales (480lb) exported

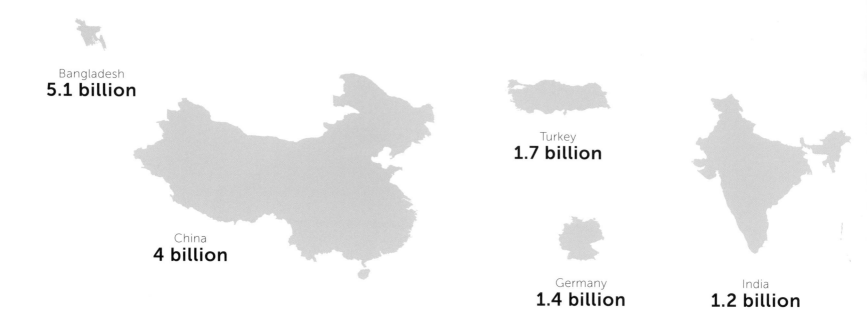

Bangladesh
5.1 billion

China
4 billion

Turkey
1.7 billion

Germany
1.4 billion

India
1.2 billion

Cotton

Whether in rural factories or urban metropolises, it is possible to manufacture clothes almost anywhere on the planet, before shipping them for display by big-name retailers in shops around the world. In this global marketplace, it is Bangladesh that has fully embraced the opportunities offered by a globalized clothing market, primarily because low minimum wages make it the ideal place for multinational corporations to quickly and cheaply produce their next fashion lines.

Bangladeshi factories owned by companies that include That's It Sportswear and Tazreen Fashion, churn out ever-increasing quantities of fabrics and textiles, to supply cheap clothing for mainstream brands. In order to cut, sew and stitch the millions and millions of dresses, shirts, trousers and t-shirts, Bangladesh requires an immense volume of cotton. Consequently it is currently the world's biggest importer of raw cotton, bringing in as much as 1.4 million tonnes a year, ahead of competing textile manufacturers such as Vietnam (1.2 million), China (1.1 million), Turkey (800,000) and Indonesia (740,000).

Such forces of globalization have transformed Bangladesh beyond imagination, in particular bringing about major financial and societal shifts in the country. This is because the cotton textiles are predominantly stitched together by Bangladeshi women; of the four million people employed in the country's textiles industry, more than 90 per cent are female. In many cases, they are the first in their families ever to take a job and gain financial autonomy of their own, creating a generation of independent, career-oriented young women.

Italy
1.1 billion

Spain
884.6 million

Vietnam
832.8 million

Netherlands
829.5 million

Honduras
823.9 million

The 10 largest exporters of cotton T-shirts, in US$. One of the leading industrial uses of cotton is in the production of t-shirts – Bangladesh are the highest exporters to high streets around the world

Perhaps surprisingly, given the end destination of a large proportion of the clothes sewn in Bangladesh, a significant volume of raw cotton is likely to travel full circle having originated in the United States. While India and China are comfortably the top two producers of cotton, the vast majority of their produce is kept within national borders for use in domestic manufacturing. In the United States, cotton growing remains a prosperous industry in Texas (8.8 million bales produced annually), Georgia (2.9 million bales) and other southern US states – huge chunks of which are for export. A whopping 3.2 million of the 3.7 million tonnes produced in the United States in 2016–17 was shipped abroad. Figures from the world's second- and third-biggest exporters of raw cotton are considerably lower than this, with 1 million tonnes coming from India and 800,000 from Australia. Worldwide, around 120 million bales of cotton are produced every single year.

Once exported, the cotton needs to be spun into yarn – a speciality of countries such as Indonesia – before being shipped on to Bangladesh. Post-manufacture, clothes are then sent on to retailers for distribution to their shops around the world. In many cases, cotton embarks on a long global journey before eventually arriving on your high street.

Food Security

Global Food Security Index overall scores by country.

25.1
Less
secure

85.6
More
secure

GFSI index

Food Security

Browsing the produce aisles in most modern supermarkets is like taking a whirlwind gastronomic journey around the world, with grains, fruits and vegetables sourced from Europe, Africa, Asia and the Americas. The globalized economy of the twenty-first century means foodstuffs can be quickly and efficiently transported from one corner of the globe to another, quite possibly being refrigerated the entire way. Human consumers can live entirely disengaged from the seasonal growing seasons that once would have been central to their daily diets, and on which they would have been wholly dependent.

In tandem with this rise of the global food network is raised awareness of food security – the degree to which a country's food supply is safe and protected from potential shocks to the system, whether natural, military or human. With large sections of a country's food supply being grown abroad and shipped across distant oceans, the reliability of the network itself has become increasingly important. The Global Food Security Network measures all countries by their food security, calculating such factors as the affordability and general availability of food, as well as the safety and nutritional value of food in each country. The top five most secure countries are Australia, Singapore, the United Kingdom, the United States and the Republic of Ireland (the Emerald Isle takes hot spot thanks to the priority the government places on large-scale domestic agriculture and an overall lack of poverty). As the index reveals, financial wealth is one of the major factors determining where a country appears on the list, far more so than geographical location.

At the bottom of the list are such countries as Sierra Leone, Chad, Madagascar, the Democratic Republic of the Congo and Burundi. These African countries suffer not only due to reduced wealth, but also to less reliable food networks. Many of their foodstuffs originate in regions of the continent frequently hit by drought, which means they have fewer reliable resources when it comes to supporting their growing, increasingly urban populations.

The London-based Royal Institute of International Affairs is an organization that seeks to raise awareness of major issues across the globe. The institute, commonly known as Chatham House, has pinpointed fourteen key 'chokepoints' that could cause havoc to the food supply to millions of people,

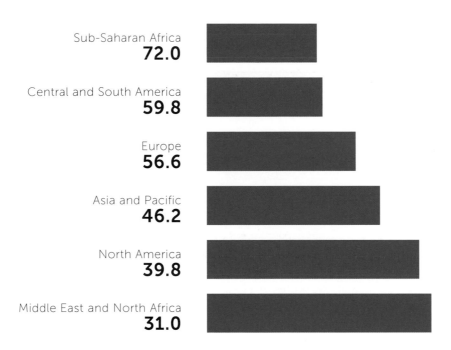

Sub-Saharan Africa
72.0

Central and South America
59.8

Europe
56.6

Asia and Pacific
46.2

North America
39.8

Middle East and North Africa
31.0

Freshwater resources risk, shown by average water indicator scores by continent. This is a measure of the health of fresh-water resources and how depletion might impact agriculture. Subindicators include water quantity and water quality risks based on agricultural water withdrawals. A higher score equals lower risk.

were they ever to be interrupted in any way. Some chokepoints are relatively obvious geographical locations – infrastructural bottlenecks, such as the Panama Canal, the Suez Canal and the Strait of Malacca, and regional pinch points such as the English Channel and Istanbul's Bosphorus, which is essential to the transportation of supplies out of the Black Sea. Other chokepoints reveal the vast numbers of people dependent on relatively unreliable transport networks, such as North America's rail network and Brazil's inland road network. The research also shows that the risks posed by these chokepoints have increased since the turn of the millennium, with the rise of unpredictable events, such as food blockades, terrorism and climate-change-related hazards. Food security is set to become an increasingly hot topic over the coming decades.

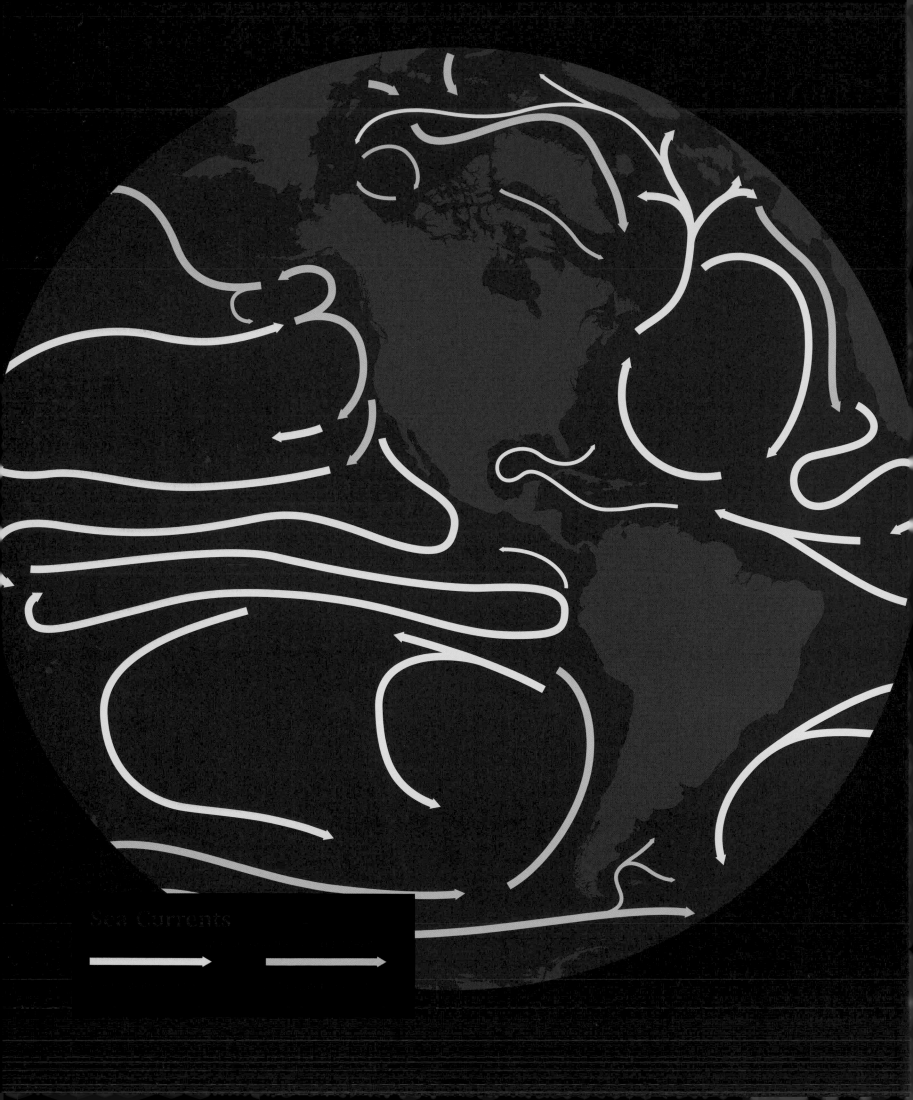

Sea Currents

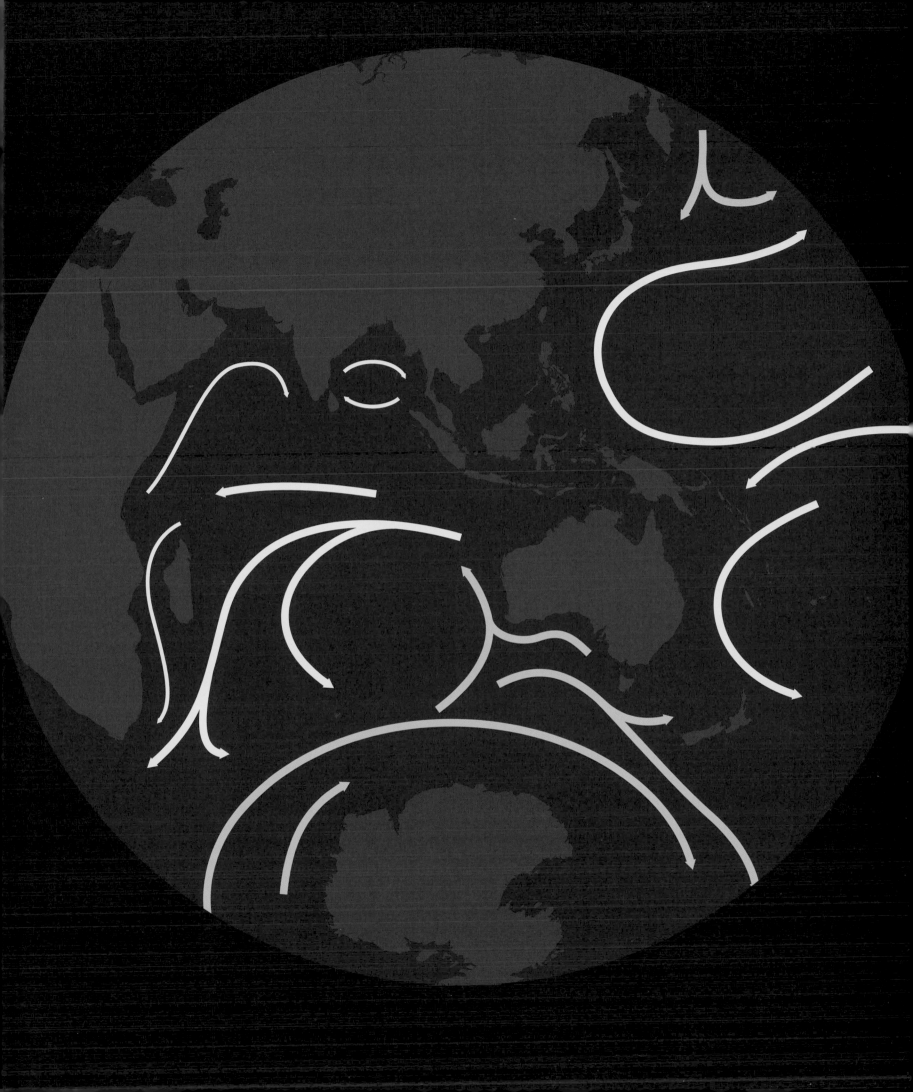

Sea Currents

Imagine an enormous flow of water, carrying up to 150 times the volume of the great Amazon River, transporting vast quantities of water across the Earth at a speed of around 5kmh (3mph). Such an entity does exist, deep below the surface of the ocean: the Gulf Stream. This powerful deep current, more than 100m (330ft) below the surface, carries warm water from the Caribbean Sea across to the other side of the North Atlantic Ocean, where it warms western Europe. This constant influx of warmth keeps the United Kingdom around 10°C (18°F) warmer than northern Canada and Siberia, which sit on roughly the same latitude. Upon reaching the North Atlantic Ocean, the current becomes cold and dense, and sinks. It then begins the process of travelling back south, down the eastern coast of South America, and into the Southern Ocean. Eventually, having circulated the globe, this water will find itself back in the Caribbean Sea, ready to jump aboard the Gulf Stream once again.

This process offers a glimpse into the operations of the global conveyor – also known as 'thermohaline circulation' – the ocean's primary method of circulating heat around the planet. Besides the Gulf Stream, the system contains such flows as the Antarctic Circumpolar Current – which keeps frozen Antarctica separated from the warm water to the north – and the California Current, which transports cool water down the Pacific coast of the United States. All in all, it takes more than one thousand years for water to complete an entire circuit of the conveyor, one of the most important large-scale natural systems in the whole world.

The conveyor is essential for transporting water around the globe, and is vital for feeding the algae and phytoplankton that form the base of the marine food chain. Studies show that up to three-quarters of all marine life is fed by nutrients circulated by the conveyor, such as South America's Humboldt current, which carries cold, nutrient-rich water from the deep ocean north towards the equator. Without the conveyor to ensure a steady replenishing of nutrients through the oceans, the microscopic creatures at the base of the food chain would cease to exist, as would the fish and larger marine creatures that prey upon them, also affecting the 500 million people worldwide who rely on fishing for their livelihoods.

Thermohaline circulation, or the Great Ocean Conveyor Belt, is the ocean's primary method of circulating heat around the planet. These deep-ocean currents are driven by differences in the water's density, which is controlled by temperature (thermos) and salinity (haline).

Unfortunately, humans could be the conveyor's undoing. Accelerating climate change is melting the Greenland ice sheet, causing billions of tonnes of ice to pour into the North Atlantic Ocean every year, diluting the warm and salty water arriving via the Gulf Stream. What might happen next is indicated by the events of 12,000 years ago, when freezing water from the melting North American icesheet arrived in the North Atlantic, slowing the conveyor so much that it triggered what is now known as the Younger Dryas. It threw the planet into deep freeze – with 'ice age'-type conditions – for up to one thousand years. Scientists warn that studies of the North Atlantic are presenting evidence that suggests meltwater from Greenland is already slowly weakening the Gulf Stream. Even slowing the conveyor, let alone halting it completely, could prevent heat being efficiently transferred around the globe, eventually changing the entire oceanic and atmospheric systems of the planet. Potentially this could lead to widespread droughts, floods, heatwaves and deep freezes, changing everything we know about what foodstuffs and other vital resources different countries can produce.

Globalization Index

KOF Globalization Index scores, by country

26.68   90.47

No data

Norway
90.43

Belgium
90.47

Italy
99.26

Globalization Index

Throngs of foreign tourists from every corner of the globe are a familiar sight on the cosmopolitan streets of Brussels, snapping photographs around the Grand Place at the centre of the Old Town, marching along Place St-Géry, the street lined with bars where drinks and dialects from all around the world flow. They might well feel at home; around 30 per cent of the population of Brussels is foreign – from the Moroccan-dominated neighbourhood of Molenbeek, to the pan-European diaspora that can be found in the bohemian Saint-Gilles district. Besides its traditional neoclassical architecture, Brussels is also home to the modern, shiny, glass buildings of the 'European Quarter', headquarters for international institutions such as the European Union and the European Parliament. On the way out towards the international Brussels airport, the administrative offices for the renowned North Atlantic Treaty Organisation (NATO) can also be found. To the north of Brussels, upstream of the Schelde River, the Flemish city of Antwerp is one of the world's major seaports, routinely frequented by cargo ship after cargo ship arriving and departing via the North Sea. Within a relatively tiny area of land, the Belgians have managed to establish robust and diverse connections to the rest of the world.

Perhaps it was for these reasons that the KOF Globalization Index named Belgium the most globalized country in the entire world. The Index compiles various social indicators (such as migration levels or the number of McDonald's), economic (such as trading relationships and levels of foreign investment) and political (such as the number of embassies and participation in international organizations) indicators to calculate their findings. The Belgians took the top spot ahead of the Netherlands, Switzerland, Sweden and Austria. There is clearly some geographical logic to these five Western European nations being the most globalized, a trend made even more obvious by Denmark, France, the United Kingdom, Germany and Finland laying claim to being the remaining top ten most globalized nations. In fact, Canada is the only non-European nation in the top twenty. Almost all of the rest are members of the European Union (EU), sharing deep political, social

The overall Globalization Index combines figures for economic, social and political globalization. Norway came top for social globalization, Singapore for economic, and Italy for political globalization, but Belgium was top of the overall charts.

Singapore
92.47

and economic ties. Or as with such countries as Switzerland and Norway, which are not EU members, belong to agreements such as the European Free Trade Association (EFTA).

Perhaps surprisingly, considering their huge sizes and massive trading relationships with other nations, though also perhaps because of these factors, the world's three biggest economies – the United States, China and Japan – sit further down the list at twenty-fourth, eighty-seventh and thirty-fifth on the rankings.

Despite rapid rises during the latter half of the twentieth century, the KOF Globalization Index shows that the overall level of globalization has barely shifted in the decade since the economic crash of 2007–08, particularly with growing protectionist policies clamping down on the movement of both people and trade across borders, and no discernable growth in political multilateralism between countries. For now, the Belgians of this world are the outliers when it comes to globalization, although perhaps the real question is, what kind of new indicators will countries be judged upon in the future, to ascertain how globalized they are?

Data credits

8-9 Data based on independent calculations from WorldsTopExports.com; 10-11 FAO, Statista; 12- 13 MasterCard (2017 Global Destination Cities Index, p2), Statista; 14-15 MasterCard (2017 Global Destination Cities Index, p3), Statista; 16-17 MasterCard (2017 Global Destination Cities Index, p2), Statista; 18-19 United Nations, Statista; 20-21 United Nations, Statista; 22-23 US Department of Agriculture; Economic Research Service (USDA - Agricultural Statistics 2017, p111-17), Statista; 24-25 Oilseeds: World Markets and Trade (March 2018), U.S. Department of Agriculture; 26-27 Quartz; Euromonitor, Statista; International Tea Committee; Deutscher Teeverband (Tee als Wirtschaftsfaktor 2017, p12), Statista; 28-29 International Tea Committee; Deutscher Teeverband (Tee als Wirtschaftsfaktor 2017, p12), Statista; 30-35 The UCS Satellite Database [www.ucsusa.org/satellite_database]; 36-37 U.S. Energy Information Administration (May 2018); BGR (2016): Energy Study 2016. reserves, resources and availability of energy resources (20). – 180 p., Hannover; 38-39 BP (BO Statistical Review of World Energy 2017, p41), Statista; 40-41 FIFA World Cup Russia 2018 List of Players; 42-43 FIFA, Statista; 44-47 Z/Yen (The Global Financial Centres Index 22), Statista; 48-51 USDA/FAS, Production, Supply and Distribution Estimates, as of March 2018; 52-55 Ofcom; Ampere Analysis (International Communications Market Report 2017, p95), Statista; 56-61 World Bank Group. 2016. Migration and Remittances Factbook 2016, Third Edition. Washington, DC: World Bank. © World Bank. https://openknowledge.worldbank.org/handle/10986/23743 License: CC BY 3.0 IGO; 62-63 Kimberley Process Certification Scheme; 66-67 Statista Consumer Market Outlook, Statista; APICCAPS (World Footwear Yearbook 2017, p115), Statista; 68-69 Statista Consumer Market Outlook, Statista; 70-73 US Geological Survey (Mineral Commodity Summaries 2018, p43), Statista; Global Cement Magazine (December 2017 issue, p17), Statista; 74-75 IMF (World Economic Outlook Database October 2017), Statista; 78-79 Stiftung Offshore-Windenergie; 4C Offshore; LORC, Statista; Global Wind Energy Council; 82-85 United Nations University (The Global E-Waste Monitor 2017), Statista; 86-89 Lloyd's List (One Hundred Ports 2017, p20), Statista; 90-93 UNOCHA, Statista; 94-97 Project Atlas, 2017, Institute of International Education; 98-99 Anderson, K, Nelgen, S, and Pinilla, V (2017). Global wine markets, 1860 to 2016: a statistical compendium. Adelaide: University of Adelaide Press. DOI: https://doi.org/10.20851/global-wine-markets. License: CC-BY 4.0; 100-101 OIV; Various sources (Trade Press) (State of the Vitiviniculture World Market 2018, p9), Statista; 102-103 Most Popular Messaging App in Every Country, ChartsBin.com, viewed 4th June, 2018, http://chartsbin.com/view/41890; 104-105 Whatsapp; Facebook (Facebook Q4 2017 Earnings Call, p4), Statista; 106-109 The Council on Tall Buildings and Urban Habitat and The Skyscraper Center; 110-111 Cochilco (Anuario de Estadisticas del Cobre y Otros Minerales 1997-2016, tabla 9), Statista; 112-113 US Geological Survey (USGS - Mineral Commodity Summaries 2018, p52), Statista; 114-119 WIPO statistics database; 120-121 FAOSTAT; 122-123 AJG Simoes, CA Hidalgo. The Economic Complexity Observatory: An Analytical Tool for Understanding the Dynamics of Economic Development. Workshops at the Twenty-Fifth AAI Conference on Artificial Intelligence. (2011); 124-127 US Geological Survey (Mineral Commodity Summaries 2018, p51), Statista; 128-131 ArtPrice.com (Contemporary Art Market 2017), Statista; 132-133 MPAA (Theatrical and Home Entertainment Report 2016, p8), Statista; European Audiovisual Observatory (Focus 2017 - World Film Market Trends, p13), Statista; 134-135 European Audiovisual Observatory (Focus 2017 - World Film Market Trends), Statista; 136-137 Consumer Market Outlook, Statista; 140-143 Department of Defense, Visual Capitalist, Statista; 144-145 Lindt & Sprüngli; Euromonitor, (Lindt & Sprüngli - Annual Report 2017, p55), Statista; FAOSTAT; 148-149 Royal FloraHolland (Royal FloraHolland Annual Report 2016), Statista; Data based on independent calculations from WorldsTopExports.com; 150-151 Royal FloraHolland (Royal FloraHolland Annual Report 2016), Statista; 152-157 CB Insights, Statista; 158-159 Inside Airbnb; 162-165 Credit Suisse (Global Wealth Databook 2017, p150), Statista; Hunrun Research Institute (Hurun Global Rich List 2017), Statista; 166-169 Early, R. et al. Global threats from invasive alien species in the twenty-first century and national response capacities. Nat. Commun. 7:12485 doi: 10.1038/ncomms12485 (2016); 170-173 FAO, Statista; GAIN; USDA Foreign Agricultural Service; GTI; GTA (Mexico Avocado Annual, p6), Statista; 174-177 www.kickstarter.com [Accessed 27/04/18]; 178-181 Federation of the Swiss Watch Industry, Statista; 182-183 FAO (FAO: pulp and paper capacities survey 2016-2021), Statista. Answers were received in time for inclusion in the survey from the following 31 countries, which represent about 80 percent of the world production of paper and paperboard: Argentina, Australia, Belgium, Brazil, Canada, Chile, China, Colombia, Czechia, Denmark, Finland, France, Germany, Hungary, Italy, Japan, Mexico, Netherlands, New Zealand, Norway, Peru, Philippines, Poland, Portugal, Russian Federation, Slovakia, Sweden, Switzerland, Thailand, United States of America and Uruguay; 186-187 WTEx; CIA (The World Factbook); International Trade Centre (Trade Map), Statista; IMF; World Gold Council, Statista; 188-189 US Geological Survey (USGS - Mineral Commodity Summaries 2018, p71), Statista; 190-191 SMMT (Motor Industry Facts 2017, p9), Statista; CAAM (cinn.cn); Sohu, Statista; 192-193 ACEA, CAAM, InsideEVs, BEA, JAMA, Statista; 194-197 WTEx,

Statista; FAOSTAT; 198-199 Newzoo (Top 50 Countries by Smartphone Users and Penetration), Statista; 200-201 Gartner, Statista; 202-203 USDA/FAS, Production, Supply and Distribution Estimates, as of March 2018; 204-205 Data based on independent calculations from WorldsTopExports.com; 206-209 The Economist (Global Food Security Index 2017), Statista; 214-217 KOF (2018 KOF Index of Globalisation), Statista

Maps and insets use the most recent data available at the time of writing, as listed below:

8-9 2016; **10-11** 2016; **12- 13** 2016; **14-15** 2016; **16-17** 2016; **18-19** 2018; **20-21** 2018; **22-23** 2016; **26-27** 2016; **28-29** 2016; **30-31** 2018; **32-33** 2018; **34-35** 2018; **36-37** 2016; **38-39** 2016; **40-41** 2018; **42-43** 2018; **44-45** 2017; **46-47** 2017; **48-49** 2017-18; **50-51** 2017-18; **52-53** 2017; **54-55** 2017; **56-57** 2016; **58-69** 2016; **60-61** 2016; **62-63** 2016; **66-67** 2017, 2016; **68-69** 2017; **70-71** 2017; **72-73** 2017; **74-75** 2016; **76-77** 2016; **78-79** 2017; **80-81** 2017; **82-83** 2016; **84-85** 2016; **86-87** 2016; **88-89** 2017, 2016; **90-91** 2017; **92-93** 2017; **94-95** 2017; **96-97** 2017; **98-99** 2016; **100-101** 2017; **102-103** 2016; **106-107** 2018; **108-109** 2018; **110-111** 2016; **112-113** 2017; **114-115** 2016; **116-117** 2017; **118-119** 2016; **120-121** 2016; **122-123** 2016; **124-125** 2017, 2016; **126-127** 2017; **128-129** 2016-17; **130-131** 2017; **132-133** 2016; **134-135** 2016; **136-137** 2017; **138-139** 2017; **140-141** 2016; **142-143** 2016; **144-145** 2017, 2016; **146-147** 2017; **148-149** 2016; **150-151** 2016; **152-153** 2018; **154-155** 2018; **156-157** 2018; **158-159** 2018; **160-161** 2018; **162-163** 2017; **164-165** 2017; **166-167** 2016; **168-169** 2016; **170-171** 2016; **172-173** 2016-17; **174-175** 2018; **176-177** 2018; **178-179** 2017; **180-181** 2017; **182-183** 2016; **184-185** 2016; **186-187** 2016, 2017; **188-189** 2017; **190-191** 2016; **192-193** 2017; **194-195** 2016; **196-197** 2016; **198-199** 2018; **202-203** 2017; **204-205** 2017; **206-207** 2017; **208-209** 2017; **214-215** 2018; **216-217** 2018

Select Bibliography

Bananas

'The imminent death of the Cavendish banana and why it affects us all', BBC News https://www.bbc.co.uk/news/uk-england-35131751

Tourism

'Defining What Makes a City a Destination, MasterCard' https://newsroom.mastercard.com/press-releases

Peacekeepers

'Troop and police contributors', United Nations Peacekeeping, https://peacekeeping.un.org/en/troop-and-police-contributors

'Why South Asia Loves Peacekeeping', *The Diplomat,* https://thediplomat.com

Soybeans

'Brazil curbs soy farming deforestation in Amazon', Reuters https://uk.reuters.com/

'Blame Henry Ford for Deadly Superbugs', Bloomberg www.bloomberg.com

Tea

Cheadle, Louise & Nick Kilby, *The Book of Tea: Growing it, making it, drinking it, the history, recipes* (2015) Jacqui Small LLP

Satellites

'This is every active satellite orbiting earth', Quartz, https://qz.com

Uranium

Amir D Aczel, *Uranium Wars: The Scientific Rivalry that Created the Nuclear Age* (2009) Palgrave Macmillan

Matteo Valleriani, *The Structures of Practical Knowledge* (2017) Springer

'How uranium ore is made into nuclear fuel', World Nuclear Association, http://www.world-nuclear.org/

Football Players

'Russia 2018 squads officially confirmed', FIFA, https://www.fifa.com/worldcup/news/russia-2018-squads-officially-confirmed

City Finances

'The Global Financial Centres Index 22, China Development Institute (CDI) and Z/YenPartners', http://www.luxembourgforfinance.com/

'Shanghai and Shenzhen stock exchanges continue to chip away at Hong Kong's IPO attractiveness', *South China Morning Post* www.scmp.com/business/

Palm Oil

'Essential oil?', *Geographical,* www.geographical.co.uk/places

'Indonesia's Fire Outbreaks Producing More Daily Emissions than Entire US Economy', World Resources Institute, https://www.wri.org/

Netflix

'Netflix's biggest competitor? Sleep', *Guardian*

'Follow Netflix's rise from tech startup to media giant rivaling Comcast', *Quartz,* https://qz.com/

Remittances

'Record high remittances to low- and middle-income countries in 2017', World Bank www.worldbank.org/

'The Money Trail', *Geographical,* www.geographical.co.uk/people

Diamonds

'A Diamond's Journey: On the cutting edge', NBC News, www.nbcnews.com/

'De Beers admits defeat over man-made diamonds', CNN, http://money.cnn.com/

Sneakers

Hinh T. Dinh, *Light Manufacturing in Vietnam: Creating Jobs and Prosperity in a Middle-Income Economy* (2014) World Bank Publications

'Vietnam's footwear industry threatened by automation', VietNamNet, http://english.vietnamnet.vn/fms/business

Cement

Robert Courland, *Concrete Planet: The Strange and Fascinating Story of the World's Most Common Man-Made Material* (2011) Prometheus Books

'Sand mining: the global environmental crisis you've probably never heard of', *Guardian,* www.theguardian.com/cities

'Sand, rarer than one thinks', UNEP, https://na.unep.net/geas/

'How seawater strengthens ancient Roman concrete', University of Utah, https://unews.utah.edu/roman-concrete/

Global Debt

'World Economic Outlook Database April 2018', International Monetary Fund, www.imf.org

Wind energy

'Is the British weather unique in the world?', BBC News, https://www.bbc.co.uk/news/magazine

Electronic Waste

'E-Waste in East and South-East Asia Jumps 63% in Five Years', UN University, https://unu.edu/media-relations

'East meets Waste: tech waste piling up in Asia', *Geographical,* www.geographical.co.uk/people/development

Ports

'Ship to shore: tracking the maritime motorways', *Geographical,* www.geographical.co.uk/places/mapping

'Lloyd's List Top 100 Ports Ranking', Maritime Intelligence, https://maritimeintelligence.informa.com/

Humanitarian Assistance

Global Humanitarian Assistance Report 2017, Development Initiatives, http://devinit.org

International Students

'Why So Many Chinese Students Come to the U.S.', *Wall Street Journal,* www.wsj.com

Wine

'A bottle of Beijing, please: is Chinese wine any good?' *Telegraph,* www.telegraph.co.uk/foodanddrink

'Wine world', *Geographical,* www.geographical.co.uk/places/mapping

Messenger Apps

'The Rags-To-Riches Tale Of How Jan Koum Built WhatsApp Into Facebook's New $19 Billion Baby', *Forbes* www.forbes.com/sites/parmyolson

Forget Apple vs. the FBI: WhatsApp just switched on encryption for a billion people, *Wired* www.wired.com

'China Blocks WhatsApp, Broadening Online Censorship', *New York Times,* www.nytimes.com/2017

'Saudi Arabia to lift ban on internet calls' Reuters, www.reuters.com

Skyscrapers

'The Skyscraper Centre', Council on Tall Buildings and Urban Habitat, www.skyscrapercenter.com

Copper

'How safe are Chile's copper mines?', BBC

News, www.bbc.co.uk/news

'Copper solution', *The Economist*, www.economist.com/business

Patents

'The International Patent System', World Intellectual Property Organization, http://www.wipo.int/pct/en/

Vanilla

'Madagascar's vanilla wars: prized spice drives death and deforestation', *Guardian*

'Vanilla shortage could lead to ice-cream price rise, makers warn', *Guardian*

Cobalt

'Democratic Republic of Congo: "This is what we die for": Human rights abuses in the Democratic Republic of the Congo power the global trade in cobalt', Amnesty International www.amnesty.org

'Carmakers and big tech struggle to keep batteries free from child labor', CNN http://money.cnn.com/

'We'll All Be Relying on Congo to Power Our Electric Cars', *Bloomberg* www.bloomberg.com

Contemporary Art

'The Contemporary Art Market Report 2017', Artprice,

www.artprice.com/artprice-reports

Cinema

'Is it a golden age for Chinese cinema?' BBC News, www.bbc.co.uk

Bottled Water

'Bottled-Water Habit Keeps Tight Grip on Mexicans', *New York Times*, www.nytimes.com

'The madness of drinking bottled water shipped halfway round the world', *Guardian*

US Military

David Vine, *Base Nation: How U.S. Military Bases Abroad Harm America and the World* (2015) Henry Holt and Company

'Comparing Aerial and Satellite Images of China's Spratly Outposts', Center for Strategic and International Studies, https://amti.csis.org/

Cocoa

'Ivory Coast sweetens up with first locally made chocolate', DW, www.dw.com

'The Chocolate Curse', Planet Money/NPR, www.npr.org/sections/money/

Flowers

'Colombia's Bloom Boom', *Slate*, www.slate.com,

'Colombia keeps cocaine from spoiling Valentine's Day flowers', *Independent*, www.independent.co.uk

Unicorns

'The Global Unicorn Club', *CB Insights*, https://www.cbinsights.com/research-unicorn-companies

Airbnb

'Airbnb's booming city neighbourhoods' *Guardian*

Airbnb, https://press.atairbnb.com/fast-facts/

Billionaires

Global Rich List 2018, Hurun Report, www.hurun.net

Invasive Species

'Global threats from invasive alien species in the twenty-first century and national response capacities', Nature Communications, www.nature.com

'Switzerland part of EU plan to battle invasive species', https://lenews.ch

Avocados

'Chilean villagers claim British appetite for avocados is draining region dry', *Guardian*

'How the Avocado Became the Fruit of Global Trade', *New York Times Magazine*

'Mexico's avocado exports to China rise', *China Daily*

Crowdfunding

The Crowd Data Centre, www.thecrowdfundingcenter.com/data/

'Fitbit formally announces that it is buying smartwatch maker Pebble', *The Verge*, www.theverge.com

Luxury Watches

'How the watch industry will save itself', *TechCrunch*, https://techcrunch.com/

'"Swiss-made" label lacks precision for watch industry', Reuters, www.reuters.com

Paper Packaging

'Finland´s forests gave it its prosperity. What will the country do in a post-paper world?', University of Helsinki, www.helsinki.fi

'Forests form the trunk of Finnish trade', Ministry for Foreign Affairs, https://finland.fi/business-innovation/forests-form-the-trunk-of-finnish-trade/

Gold

'Mnuchin's Fort Knox Quip: 'I Assume the Gold Is Still There',' Bloomberg www.bloomberg.com

Fort Knox Bullion Depository, United States Mint,

www.usmint.gov/about/mint-tours-facilities/fort-knox

Car Exports

'Who Invented the Car?', Live Science, www.livescience.com

'Iran Automotive Industry -- Can American Car Manufacturers Overcome Chinese Resistance?', Forbes, www.forbes.com

'China's Car Revolution Is Going Global', Bloomberg, www.bloomberg.com/

'Power to the EV: Norway spearheads Europe's electric vehicle surge', *Guardian*

Honey

Ghosh G K, *Beekeeping in India* (1994) APH Publishing

Ethel Eva Crane, *The World History of Beekeeping and Honey Hunting* (1999) Taylor & Francis

Smartphone Users

'First Smartphone Turns 20: Fun Facts About Simon', *Time*

Cotton

'Despite Low Pay, Poor Work Conditions, Garment Factories Empowering Millions Of Bangladeshi Women', *International Business Times*, www.ibtimes.com

Food Security

'Chokepoints and Vulnerabilities in Global Food Trade', Chatham House, www.chathamhouse.org

Global Food Security Index 2017, Economist Intelligence Unit, https://foodsecurityindex.eiu.com

Sea Currents

'The Global Conveyor Belt', National Oceanic and Atmospheric Administration https://oceanservice.noaa.gov

Globalization Index

KOF Globalization Index, ETH Zurich www.kof.ethz.ch

Index

Chris Fitch is senior staff writer at Geographical, the official magazine of the Royal Geographical Society (with IBG), and author of *Atlas of Untamed Places: An extraordinary journey through our wild world*, nominated for a 2018 Edward Stanford Travel Writing Award.

@christophfitch chrisfitch.co.uk

Sam Vickars is a data visualization designer and engineer. He earned his Masters of Science in Data Visualization from Parsons School of Design in New York City, and has worked with the United Nations Development Programme and the National Centre for Truth and Reconciliation. Sam lives in Vancouver, Canada, where he continues to tell meaningful stories with data.

samvickars.com

Many thanks to Lucy Warburton, Emma Harverson and the rest of the team at White Lion Publishing, without whom this book would never have existed. Their enthusiasm for the project drove us forward constantly, and the final product is a tribute to their hard work and dedication.

I'm very grateful to Sam Vickars for turning some very complicated and diverse data into a range of diverse and engaging maps, cleverly capturing the unique stories behind each entry. Equally, many thanks to Paileen Currie for designing a book that feels rich with detail, to Anna Southgate for her copyedit and to Victoria Lyle for proofreading and double-checking the many, many facts included in the book. Finally, many thanks to all my family, friends, and colleagues for their ongoing and tireless support.